AQA

Biology for GCSE Combined Science: Trilogy

Foundation Workbook

Gemma Young
Editor: Lawrie Ryan

OXFORD
UNIVERSITY PRESS

OXFORD
UNIVERSITY PRESS

Great Clarendon Street, Oxford, OX2 6DP, United Kingdom

Oxford University Press is a department of the University of Oxford.
It furthers the University's objective of excellence in research,
scholarship, and education by publishing worldwide. Oxford is a
registered trade mark of Oxford University Press in the UK and in
certain other countries

© Oxford University Press 2017

The moral rights of the authors have been asserted

First published in 2017

British Library Cataloguing in Publication Data
Data available

978 0 19 835934 0

10 9 8 7

Paper used in the production of this book is a natural, recyclable
product made from wood grown in sustainable forests.
The manufacturing process conforms to the environmental regulations
of the country of origin.

Printed in Great Britain by CPI Group (UK) Ltd., Croydon CR0 4YY

COVER: ETHAN DANIELS/SCIENCE PHOTO LIBRARY

p11(T) John Durham/Science Photo Library

p105(T) Wim van Egmond/Science Photo Library

All artwork by Q2A media

Contents

Any topics omitted from your workbook and from this contents page are Higher tier.

Introduction

Practice activities – Lots of varied questions, increasing in difficulty, to build your confidence and help you progress through the course

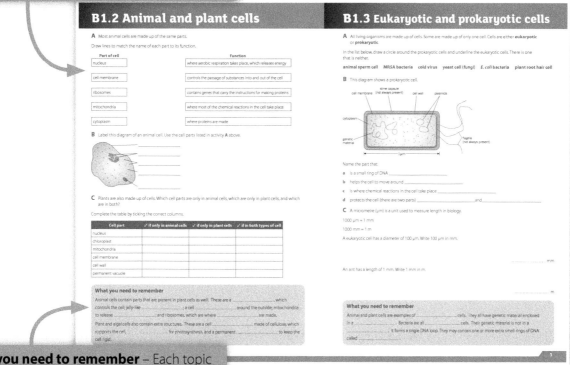

What you need to remember – Each topic from your GCSE Student Book is covered, and includes a summary of the key content you need to know

Hints – Handy hints to give you extra guidance on how to answer more complex questions

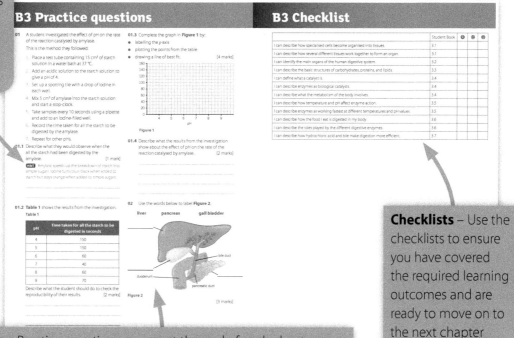

Checklists – Use the checklists to ensure you have covered the required learning outcomes and are ready to move on to the next chapter

Practice questions – Practice questions appear at the end of each chapter, to test your knowledge. They include a mix of short and long-answer question types, as well as practical-focused questions so you can practise the key skills required for your examinations. All answers are in the Workbook, allowing for instant feedback and self-assessment

B1.1 The world of the microscope

A A light microscope is used to magnify objects.

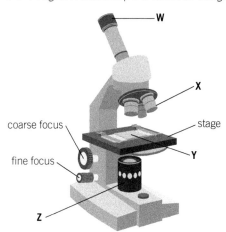

Match each missing label on the diagram to the correct word below.

Write **W**, **X**, **Y**, or **Z** beside each word.

slide ☐

eyepiece lens ☐

objective lens ☐

light ☐

B Another type of microscope is the electron microscope.

Circle **true** or **false** for each statement.

a Electron microscopes have a higher magnification than light microscopes.   **true/false**

b Electron microscopes can be used to study live specimens.   **true/false**

c Light microscopes were invented before electron microscopes.   **true/false**

d Light microscopes are rarely used by scientists.   **true/false**

C You can calculate the size of an object viewed under a microscope by using the formula:

$$\text{size of real object} = \frac{\text{size of image}}{\text{magnification}}$$

A student uses a magnification of ×100 to view a cell. The diameter of the image is 10 mm.

Calculate the diameter of the cell.

_____

What you need to remember

Microscopes can make objects look bigger – they _____ them. You need a microscope to see cells because they are too _____ to see with just your eyes. Light microscopes use a beam of light to form an image of an object. Electron microscopes use a beam of _____ .
Electron microscopes have a higher _____ than light microscopes. They also have a higher _____ power, which means they show magnified objects in more detail. However, electron microscopes are much _____ than light microsopes, and are _____ expensive.

B1.2 Animal and plant cells

A Most animal cells are made up of the same parts.

Draw lines to match the name of each part to its function.

Part of cell		Function
nucleus		where aerobic respiration takes place, which releases energy
cell membrane		controls the passage of substances into and out of the cell
ribosomes		contains genes that carry the instructions for making proteins
mitochondria		where most of the chemical reactions in the cell take place
cytoplasm		where proteins are made

B Label this diagram of an animal cell. Use the cell parts listed in activity **A** above.

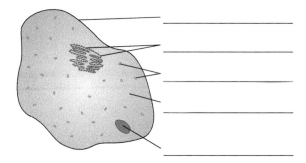

C Plants are also made up of cells. Which cell parts are only in animal cells, which are only in plant cells, and which are in both?

Complete the table by ticking the correct columns.

Cell part	✓ if only in animal cells	✓ if only in plant cells	✓ if in both types of cell
nucleus			
chloroplast			
mitochondria			
cell membrane			
cell wall			
permanent vacuole			

What you need to remember

Animal cells contain parts that are present in plant cells as well. These are a _____, which controls the cell; jelly-like _____; a cell _____ around the outside; mitochondria to release _____; and ribosomes, which are where _____ are made.

Plant and algal cells also contain extra structures. These are a cell _____ made of cellulose, which supports the cell, _____ for photosynthesis, and a permanent _____ to keep the cell rigid.

B1.3 Eukaryotic and prokaryotic cells

A All living organisms are made up of cells. Some are made up of only one cell. Cells are either **eukaryotic** or **prokaryotic**.

In the list below, draw a circle around the prokaryotic cells and underline the eukaryotic cells. There is one that is neither.

animal sperm cell   MRSA bacteria   cold virus   yeast cell (fungi)   *E. coli* bacteria   plant root hair cell

B This diagram shows a prokaryotic cell.

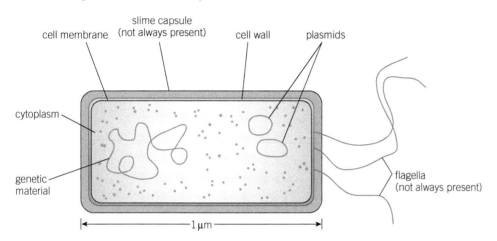

Name the part that:

a is a small ring of DNA _____

b helps the cell to move around _____

c is where chemical reactions in the cell take place _____

d protects the cell (there are two parts) _____and_____

C A micrometre (μm) is a unit used to measure length in biology.

1000 μm = 1 mm

1000 mm = 1 m

A eukaryotic cell has a diameter of 100 μm. Write 100 μm in mm.

_____ mm

An ant has a length of 1 mm. Write 1 mm in m.

_____ m

What you need to remember

Animal and plant cells are examples of _____ cells. They all have genetic material enclosed in a _____ . Bacteria are all _____ cells. Their genetic material is not in a _____ . It forms a single DNA loop. They may contain one or more extra small rings of DNA called _____ .

B1.4 Specialisation in animal cells

A A nerve cell is an example of a **specialised cell**.

What are specialised cells?

Tick the correct box.

W They are special cells, found only in humans. ☐

X They have special features to allow them to carry out a function. ☐

Y They are found only in the nervous system. ☐

Z They are very long cells. ☐

B Draw a line to match each specialised cell to its function.

Cell	Function
nerve cell	contracts and relaxes to help movement
muscle cell	carries electrical impulses around the body
sperm cell	contains genetic information from the male parent

C This diagram shows a sperm cell.

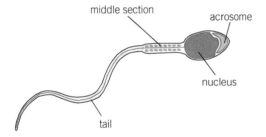

Finish the sentences to explain how it is specialised to carry out its function:

a To move through the female reproductive system and reach the egg, the sperm has a _____ .

b The middle section is full of mitochondria to provide _____ .

c The acrosome contains digestive enzymes to _____ .

d The nucleus contains _____

_____ .

What you need to remember

As an organism develops, cells _____ to form different types of cell. A _____ cell

has different structures to enable it to carry out a certain _____ . Examples of specialised animal

cells are _____ cells, which carry electrical impulses; _____ cells for movement;

and sperm cells, which fertilise an _____ cell.

B1.5 Specialisation in plant cells

A LIke animals, plants have specialised cells – cells with particular structures to allow them to carry out a function. These special structures are called adaptations.

Here are diagrams of three specialised plant cells. Write the name of each cell under the diagrams.

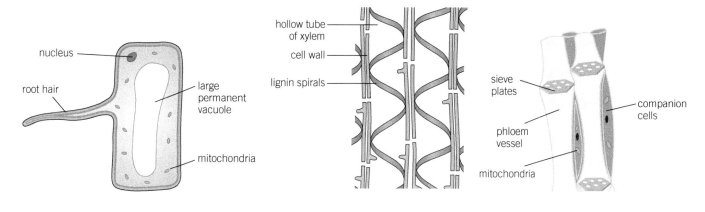

_____   _____   _____

B Draw lines to match each specialised cell to one of its adaptations and how this helps it to perform its function.

Specialised cell	Adaptation	How it helps
phloem cell	increased surface area	allows dissolved food to move up and down the stem
xylem cell	sieve plates	increases the amount of water that the plant can absorb
root hair cell	rings of lignin	helps withstand the pressure of water

C Photosynthetic cells are cells in a plant that carry out photosynthesis.

Circle **true** or **false** for the following statements about photosynthetic cells.

a They are found in all parts of the plant.   **true/false**

b They contain many chloroplasts.   **true/false**

c They do not have a cell wall.   **true/false**

d They are usually positioned in layers.   **true/false**

What you need to remember

Plant cells may be _____ to carry out a particular function. Root hair cells are one example. They have a large surface _____ to increase water absorption. Xylem and phloem cells are involved in transporting substances around the plant. Xylem transports _____ and dissolved mineral ions. It is made up of tubes strengthened with _____ . Phloem carries dissolved food. _____ plates at the ends of the cells allow this to move freely up and down the tubes.

B1.6 Diffusion

A Many substances move in and out of cells by **diffusion**.

Use the words below to fill the gaps in this explanation of diffusion.

net   **gas**   **higher**   **random**   **concentration**   **solute**

Diffusion is the spreading out of the particles of a _____, or of any substance in solution (a _____).

This results in the _____ movement (overall movement) of particles.

The net movement is from an area of _____ concentration to an area of lower _____ of the particle.

It takes place because of the _____ movement of the particles. The motion of the particles causes them to bump into each other, and this moves them all around.

B The diagrams below show diffusion taking place, but they are in the wrong order.

P	Q	R	S

Write the letters in the boxes below to show the correct order.

C In your lungs, oxygen diffuses from the air into the bloodstream.

In the table below, each change will speed up or slow down the rate (speed) of diffusion.
Complete the table by ticking the correct columns.

Change	✓ if rate increases	✓ if rate decreases
increase in air temperature		
blood moving more quickly		
make the lungs smaller		
more oxygen in the air		

What you need to remember

Diffusion is the spreading out of particles, resulting in a net _____ from an area

of _____ concentration to an area of _____ concentration. The

_____ of diffusion is affected by the difference in concentration (the concentration

_____), the temperature, and the available surface _____ . Substances move

in and out of cells by diffusion. Examples are glucose, urea, and gases such as _____ and

carbon dioxide.

B1.7 Osmosis

A Osmosis is a special type of diffusion. Circle the correct **bold** words in the paragraph below.

Osmosis is the movement of **water/any soluble substance** from a dilute to a more **dilute/concentrated** solution

through a **partially/totally** permeable **membrane/cell wall** that allows water to pass through.

B Draw an arrow on the diagram to show the net movement of water molecules.

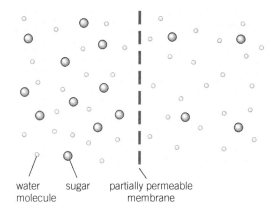

water molecule   sugar   partially permeable membrane

C Some scientists put three different animal cells in solutions containing different concentrations of glucose.

Tick the columns to show if the solutions outside the cells are **isotonic**, **hypertonic**, or **hypotonic**.

Cell	Concentration of glucose inside the cell in g/dm³	Concentration of glucose in the solution outside the cell in g/dm³	✓ if solution is isotonic	✓ if solution is hypertonic	✓ if solution is hypotonic
X	0.5	0.1			
Y	0.8	1.2			
Z	0.4	0.4			

D Describe what the scientists would see happen to cells **X** and **Y** from activity **C** above.

cell **X** _____

cell **Y** _____

What you need to remember

Osmosis is a special type of _____ . It is the movement of _____ from a dilute

solution to a more _____ solution through a partially permeable _____ .

_____ moves into or out of a cell by osmosis if there are solutions of different concentrations

inside and outside the cell.

- If the concentration of the solution is the _____ as the concentration of the inside of the cell

  then the solution is isotonic.

- If the concentration of the solution is higher than the concentration of the inside of the cell then the

  solution is _____ .

- If the concentration of the solution is lower than the concentration of the inside of the cell then the

  solution is _____ .

B1.8 Osmosis in plants

A Water enters and leaves plant cells by osmosis. The amount of water in the cell affects the structure of the cell.

Draw a line to match each diagram to the word that describes the cell.

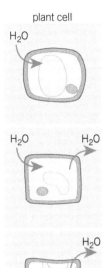

plant cell

plasmolysed

turgid (normal)

flaccid

B Marco investigated osmosis in potato cells.

He placed discs of potato in different concentrations of sugar solution. He then left them for 30 minutes.

He measured the percentage change in mass and plotted his results on a graph.

a Draw a line of best fit.

b One of the results is anomalous (looks wrong). Circle it.

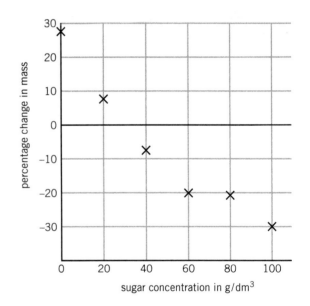

C Circle the correct **bold** words to complete Marco's conclusion.

At sugar solutions of 0 and 20 g/dm³ the mass of the potato discs **increased/decreased** because there was a net movement of water **into/out of** the potato cells.

At sugar solutions of 40 g/dm³ and above the mass of the potato discs **increased/decreased** because there was a net movement of water **into/out of** the potato cells.

I can tell from the graph that at a concentration of around **30/40** g/dm³ there was no movement of water in or out of the cells. This is because the concentration of sugar inside the potato cells was **different from/the same as** the surrounding solution.

What you need to remember

Osmosis is important to maintain pressure called _____ in plant cells. This keeps the cells rigid. If a plant cell _____ water it becomes _____ (soft). This causes the plant to wilt. If a cell loses a lot of water the cell _____ pulls away from the cell wall. This is called _____ .

B1.9 Active transport

A Active transport is another way in which substances are moved in and out of cells.

Draw a line to match the start of each sentence to its end.

Active transport moves substances from...	...many mitochondria for energy release.
Cells involved in active transport normally have...	...a more dilute solution to a more concentrated solution.
One use of active transport is for the movement of...	...the concentration gradient.
Active transport moves substances against...	...glucose from the gut into the bloodstream.

B Which of the following uses active transport? Tick the correct box.

X oxygen moving from the lungs into the bloodstream ☐

Y mineral ions moving from the soil into plant roots ☐

Z carbon dioxide moving from a leaf into the air ☐

C Describe what this graph shows.

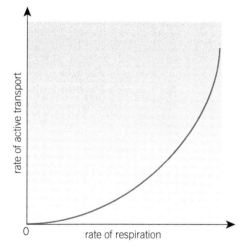

_____

_____

What you need to remember

Active transport moves substances from a more _____ solution to a more concentrated solution.
This is against a concentration _____ .

Active transport uses energy released from food during _____ . Plant _____
hairs absorb mineral ions from very dilute solutions in the _____ using active transport. Active
transport also enables sugar molecules to be absorbed from lower concentrations in the gut into the blood,
where the concentration of sugar is _____ .

B1.10 Exchanging materials

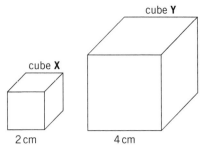

cube Y

cube X

2 cm   4 cm

A The surface area to volume ratio (SA : V ratio) is very important in biology.

A student measured the surface area to volume ratio of some different-sized cubes.

Complete the gaps in the table.

Cube	Length of one side in cm	Area of one side in cm²	Total area of all sides in cm²	Volume in cm³	SA : V ratio
Example	1	1	6	1	6 : 1
X	2	4		8	
Y	4		96		1.5 : 1

B Use the words below to fill the gaps.

gases   exchange   smaller   waste   bigger   diffusion

As living organisms get bigger, their surface area to volume ratio gets _____.

This makes it more difficult to _____ materials quickly enough with the outside world.

_____ and food molecules can no longer reach every cell inside the organism by _____.

Metabolic _____ cannot be removed fast enough to avoid poisoning the cells.

C Your lungs contain millions of tiny air sacs (alveoli) where gas exchange takes place between the air and the blood.

The diagram opposite shows a group of alveoli.

Name **one** way in which alveoli are adapted for effective gas exchange.

_____

_____

_____

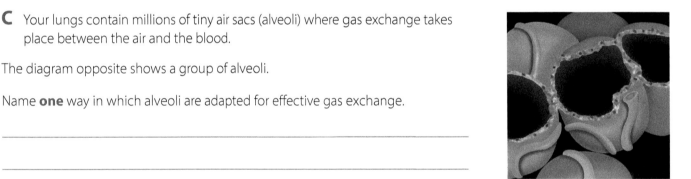

What you need to remember

Single-celled organisms have a relatively _____ surface area to volume ratio. As a cell increases in size, the surface area to volume ratio _____ .

Multicellular organisms have special surfaces where exchange of materials takes place.

Exchange surfaces usually have a _____ surface area and _____ walls, which give short diffusion distances. Examples in plants are roots and leaves. In animals, exchange surfaces also have an efficient _____ supply. Examples include gills in _____ and alveoli in humans.

B1 Practice questions

01 **Figure 1** shows a leaf from a water plant called *Elodea* viewed under a light microscope.

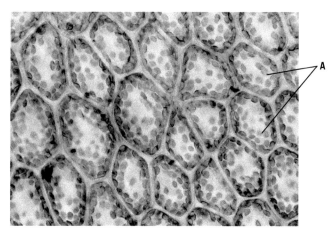

Figure 1

01.1 The cells contain many small green structures. These are labelled **A** on **Figure 1**.

What are they called?

Tick **one** box. [1 mark]

HINT They are green because they contain chlorophyll.

X mitochondria ☐

Y vacuoles ☐

Z chloroplasts ☐

01.2. The objective lens to view the *Elodea* has a magnification of ×4. The magnification of the eyepiece lens is ×10.

Calculate the total magnification used. [2 marks]

HINT total magnification = magnification of eyepiece lens × magnification of objective lens.

_____

_____

_____

02 Placing plant tissue in sugar solution may cause water to enter or leave the tissue.

02.1 Name the transport process involved in the movement of water across a cell membrane.

[1 mark]

HINT This is a special type of diffusion in which water moves from a higher to a lower concentration.

_____

02.2 A group of students was asked to carry out an experiment to show how the concentration of sugar solution affects how much water enters or leaves the cell by the process identified in **02.1**.

Write a suitable method. Include the **equipment** they could use. [6 marks]

HINT Consider what they need to change (the independent variable) and measure (the dependent variable). How could they measure the dependent variable?

_____

_____

_____

_____

_____

_____

_____

_____

_____

_____

03 **Figure 2** shows a plant cell.

Figure 2

03.1 Name this cell. [1 mark]

_____

03.2 Explain how it is adapted for its function. [3 marks]

_____

_____

_____

_____

B1 Checklist

	Student Book	🙂	😐	☹
I can describe how microscopy techniques have developed over time.	1.1			
I can explain the differences in magnification and resolution between a light microscope and an electron microscope.	1.1			
I can calculate the magnification, real size, and image size of a specimen.	1.1			
I can identify the main parts of animal cells.	1.2			
I can describe the similarities and differences between plant and animal cells.	1.2			
I can describe the similarities and differences between eukaryotic cells and prokaryotic cells.	1.3			
I can explain how bacteria compare with animal and plant cells.	1.3			
I can describe the size and scale of cells using order of magnitude calculations.	1.3			
I can describe how cells differentiate to form specialised cells.	1.4			
I can explain how animal cells may be specialised to carry out a particular function.	1.4			
I can describe how the structure of different types of animal cells relates to their function.	1.4			
I can explain how plant cells may be specialised to carry out a particular function.	1.5			
I can describe how the structure of different types of plant cells relates to their function.	1.5			
I can describe how diffusion takes place and why it is important in living organisms.	1.6			
I can describe what affects the rate of diffusion.	1.6			
I can compare and contrast osmosis and diffusion.	1.7			
I can explain why osmosis is important in animal cells.	1.7			
I can explain why osmosis is important in plant cells.	1.8			
I can describe an investigation into the effect of osmosis on plant tissues.	1.8			
I can describe how active transport works.	1.9			
I can explain the importance of active transport in cells.	1.9			
I can describe how the surface area to volume ratio varies depending on the size of an organism.	1.10			
I can explain why large multicellular organisms need special systems for exchanging materials with the environment.	1.10			

B2.1 Cell division

A Genetic material is found in your cells.

Draw a line to match the name of each part to its function.

Part		Function
gene		part of the cell where genetic material is found
cell		a string of many genes
chromosome		a small piece of DNA that controls a characteristic
nucleus		what living organisms are made up of

B These statements are about chromosomes and cell division.

Circle **true** or **false** for each statement.

a   Human body cells contain 23 pairs of chromosomes.   **true/false**

b   Sperm and egg cells contain 46 chromosomes. **true/false**

c   The purpose of cell division is to halve the number of chromosomes in cells. **true/false**

d   During cell division DNA is replicated. **true/false**

C Tick any boxes that show a function of mitotic cell division.

W to produce new cells for growth ☐

X to destroy old cells ☐

Y to replace worn-out skin cells ☐

Z to produce offspring in asexual reproduction ☐

What you need to remember

Body cells divide in a series of stages called the cell _____ . During the cell cycle the genetic material is doubled. One set of chromosomes is pulled to each end of the cell. The nucleus divides into _____ identical nuclei in a process called _____ . Finally the cytoplasm and cell membranes divide to form two identical cells.

Mitotic cell division is important in the growth, _____ , and development of multicellular organisms.

B2.2 Growth and differentiation

A As cells divide, grow, and develop they **differentiate**.

Draw a line to match the start of each sentence to its end.

Embryos contain stem cells, which are...	...genes are switched on or off.
Stem cells can become...	...specialised.
Most adult cells are...	...unspecialised.
During the process of differentiation...	...any type of cell.

B This activity is about the stem cells in plants and animals.

Complete the table by ticking the correct columns.

Statement	✓ if true for animals only	✓ if true for plants only	✓ if true for both plants and animals
contains stem cells			
growth happens throughout life			
differentiation is permanent			
stem cells are found in several different places			
stem cells are found only in regions called meristems			

C Circle **one** part of the plant root in the diagram to show where stem cells are found.

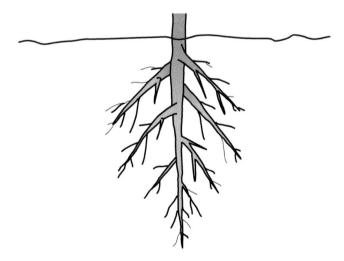

What you need to remember

Stem cells are unspecialised and have the ability to _____ into many different types of cell.

In animals they are found in _____ and in some places in adults.

In plant cells, new unspecialised cells are formed in the _____ found in the shoot and _____ tips. They then differentiate. This process takes place throughout the plant's life.

B2.3 Stem cells

A In an adult human body, which tissue is a good source of stem cells?

Tick **one** box.

T bone marrow ☐

U heart ☐

V stomach ☐

B Which conditions could be treated by using stem cells?

Tick **two** boxes.

W paralysis ☐

X cancer ☐

Y type 1 diabetes ☐

Z malaria ☐

C Stem cells from plant tissues called meristems can be used to produce clones of plants. The plants are produced quickly and economically.

Name **one** other advantage of using this method to grow new plants.

_____

What you need to remember

Embryonic and _____ stem cells can be cloned and made to differentiate into many different types of cell. Treatment with stem cells may be able to help conditions such as paralysis and _____ .

Stem cells from plant _____ are used to produce new plant clones. They can be grown _____ and cheaply and are used for research and farming.

B2.4 Stem cell dilemmas

A Scientists are researching the use of embryonic stem cells to cure some diseases. The diagram opposite shows how this works.

Write the letters for the statements below in the correct boxes to label the diagram.

V The stem cells are made to differentiate into different types of specialised cell.

W The stem cells are cloned.

X An early human embryo is grown in a dish.

Y Tissues or organs made up of specialised cells are transplanted into the patient.

Z Stem cells are removed from the embryo.

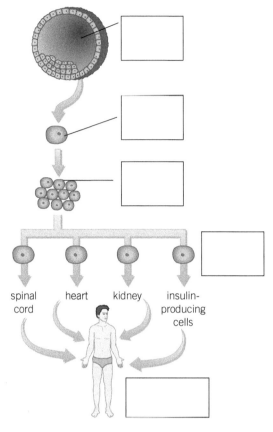

spinal cord   heart   kidney   insulin-producing cells

B Using human stem cells for medical treatments is a new technology. There are issues associated with it.

Read the following information.

> Stem cells are taken from embryos. The embryos will be destroyed after being used.
>
> Stem cells divide and grow quickly. There is some concern that using embryonic stem cells to treat people might cause cancer.
>
> Some research has shown the potential of stem cells to treat conditions such as paralysis and diabetes.
>
> However, progress in developing these therapies has been relatively slow, difficult, and expensive. Some people feel that this money would be better spent on research into other areas of medicine.

a Draw a blue circle around a benefit of stem cell research.

b Draw a red circle around a possible risk.

c Draw a box around an ethical concern.

d Underline an economic concern.

What you need to remember

The use of embryonic stem cells in medicine has potential benefits but also has some _____ as well as _____ , social, and economic issues. In _____ cloning, an embryo is produced with the same genes as the patient. The patient does not _____ the stem cells so they may be used for a medical treatment. Scientists are also researching ways of using _____ stem cells in medicine.

B2 Practice questions

01 Choose from the words below to complete the information about chromosomes. [2 marks]

HINT Chromosomes contain DNA – the genetic material of cells.

DNA cytoplasm genes nucleus pairs of single

Chromosomes are found in the _____ of a cell.

Each chromosome carries a large number of _____, which are made of the molecule _____.

Human body cells contain 23 _____ chromosomes.

02 Look at **Figure 1**.

Figure 1

02.1 Which process (**A** or **B**) is mitosis? [1 mark]

_____

02.2 Explain how you decided. [1 mark]

HINT Mitosis is a type of cell division in which the DNA is replicated (copied).

_____

_____

_____

03 **Figure 2** opposite shows one way in which scientists hope embryonic stem cells might be used in medical treatments in the future.

early human embryo formed from the patient's genes

stem cells removed

stem cells cultured

stem cells made to differentiate into different tissues

spinal cord   heart   kidney   insulin-producing cells

organs or tissues transplanted into a patient to cure them

Figure 2

03.1 What is the name of this medical treatment? Tick **one** box. [1 mark]

W transplantation ☐

X therapeutic cloning ☐

Y embryonic cloning ☐

Z stem cell treatment ☐

03.2 Name **one** condition that could be treated in this way. [1 mark]

_____

03.3 Give **two** reasons why embryonic stem cells are used for this treatment. [2 marks]

HINT Embryonic stem cells are able to differentiate into any type of cell. These can be used to replace cells in people affected by illnesses.

1. _____

2. _____

03.4 Describe **one** ethical objection some people have to this treatment. [1 mark]

_____

_____

B2 Checklist

	Student Book	☺	☻	☹
I can describe the role of the chromosomes in cells.	2.1			
I can explain the importance of the cell cycle.	2.1			
I can describe how cells divide by mitosis.	2.1			
I can compare and contrast cell differentiation in animals and plants.	2.2			
I can describe how plant clones are produced and their uses.	2.2			
I can compare stem cells to other body cells.	2.3			
I can describe the functions of stem cells in embryos, in adult animals, and in plants.	2.3			
I can describe how treatment with stem cells may be used to treat people with different medical conditions.	2.3			
I can describe the process of therapeutic cloning.	2.4			
I can evaluate some of the potential benefits, risks, and social and ethical issues of the use of stem cells in medical research and treatments.	2.4			

B3.1 Tissues and organs

A The cells of multicellular organisms are organised into levels.

Write the terms below to complete the diagram showing how they are organised.

| organs | whole body | organ systems | tissues |

cells ⇒ ⬭ ⇒ ⬭ ⇒ ⬭ ⇒ ⬭

B The stomach is an organ made up of several different tissues.

Draw a line to match each type of tissue to its function in the stomach.

Tissue

| muscular | | helps churn the food and digestive juices together |

| glandular | | covers the inside and outside of the organ |

| epithelial | | produces digestive juices that break down food |

Function

C Name the organ systems shown in the diagram below.

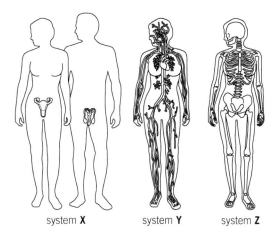

system **X**   system **Y**   system **Z**

system **X** _____

system **Y** _____

system **Z** _____

What you need to remember

A tissue is a group of _____ with similar structures and functions. An example is _____
tissue, which can contract to bring about movement. Organs are collections of _____ performing
specific functions. The _____ is an organ involved in the digestion of food. It is made up of
muscular, epithelial, and _____ tissue. Organs are organised into organ _____ , which
work together to form organisms. The stomach is part of the _____ system.

B3.2 The human digestive system

A Here is a diagram of the human digestive system.

Use the words below to label the diagram.

stomach

liver

small intestine

gullet

large intestine

mouth
(containing teeth, tongue, and salivary glands)

diaphragm

gall bladder

duodenum

bile duct

appendix

pancreas

rectum

anus

B Write down what part of the digestive system is being described in each of the following statements.

a Where undigested food (faeces) leaves the body. _____

b Intestine where water is absorbed from undigested food. _____

c Muscular bag where food is mixed with digestive juices. _____

d Gland that produces digestive enzymes that are released into the duodenum. _____

e Muscular tube that squeezes food from the mouth into the stomach. _____

f Where food enters the body. _____

g Produces bile. _____

h Intestine where small, soluble food molecules are absorbed into the bloodstream. _____

What you need to remember

The _____ system in a mammal is an organ system where several _____ work together to digest and absorb food. During digestion large _____ food molecules are broken down into _____ soluble molecules that can enter the _____ .

B3.3 The chemistry of food

A Complete the table to show information about carbohydrates, lipids, and proteins.

Food molecule	One food that is a good source	Use in the body
carbohydrates	pasta	
	olive oil	
		forming new tissues, enzymes, and hormones

B Choose from the words below to label the diagrams of food molecules.

glucose **lipid** **amino acid** **protein** **sucrose**

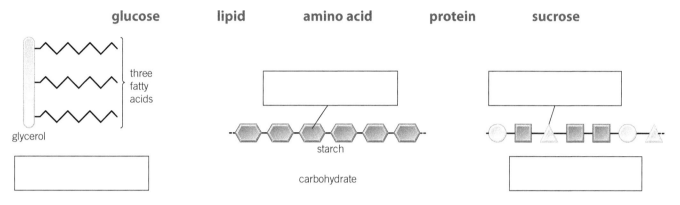

C You can test foods to find out what food molecules they contain.

Draw lines to connect the food being tested to the reagent used and the result if the molecule is present.

Food molecule	Reagent to use	Result if food being tested contains the molecule
starch	ethanol	blue-black colour
simple sugar (e.g., glucose)	blue Benedict's solution	purple colour
protein	orange iodine solution	cloudy, white layer
lipid	blue Biuret solution	brick-red colour

What you need to remember

Carbohydrates, _____, and lipids are food molecules. They are made up of smaller molecules joined together. Simple sugars are carbohydrates that contain only one or two sugar units. Complex carbohydrates, such as _____, contain long chains of simple sugar units bonded together. Lipids consist of three molecules of fatty acids bonded to a molecule of _____. Protein molecules are made up of long chains of _____ acids.

B3.4 Catalysts and enzymes

A Enzymes are biological catalysts.

Define a catalyst.

_____

B Some enzymes are used to break up large molecules.

Circle the correct **bold** words in the sentences below to show how this works. Use the diagram to help you.

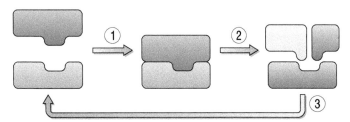

The **substrate/product** fits into the **reaction/active** site on the enzyme. This is called the **ball and ring/lock and key** theory.

The substrate is split up into **reactants/products**, which leave the enzyme.

The **substrate/enzyme** is ready to use again.

C A student wanted to find out which catalyst would break down hydrogen peroxide at the fastest rate.

They planned to use a powder called manganese(IV) oxide and an enzyme called catalase in the equipment shown below.

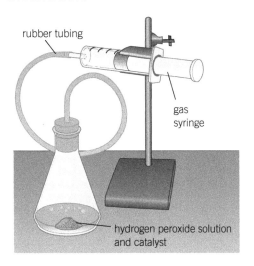

rubber tubing

gas syringe

hydrogen peroxide solution and catalyst

Tick the boxes to show the types of variables they will use.

	✓ if independent variable	✓ if dependent variable	✓ if control variable
mass of catalyst			
volume of hydrogen peroxide			
volume of gas produced over time			
temperature of catalyst			
type of catalyst			

What you need to remember

Enzymes are biological _____ . They increase the _____ of chemical reactions inside living organisms. Enzymes are proteins. The _____ acid chains are folded to form the _____ site, which matches the shape of a specific _____ molecule. This is called the lock and _____ theory. Enzymes control _____ , the sum of all the reactions in a cell or the body. They speed up reactions, such as building large molecules from _____ ones, _____ down large molecules, and changing one molecule into another.

A An enzyme is added to a solution of substrate.

Which factors affect the rate of the reaction?

Tick as many boxes as you need.

S temperature of the mixture ☐

T concentration of the substrate solution ☐

U size of the enzyme molecules ☐

V pH of the solution ☐

B This graph shows the rate of an enzyme-controlled reaction.

Circle the correct **bold** temperatures in the paragraph below to explain what it shows.

Between **0/10** °C and **37/54** °C the rate of reaction increases with the increase in temperature.

37/54 °C is the optimum temperature, at which the reaction works as fast as possible.

Higher than **10/37** °C the rate of reaction decreases with the increase in temperature.

At around **41/54** °C and over the enzyme stops working.

C Why do enzymes stop working over a certain temperature?

Tick the correct box.

W The active site changes shape. ☐

X The enzyme dies. ☐

Y The enzyme melts. ☐

Z The substrate evaporates. ☐

What you need to remember

Enzyme activity is affected by _____ and pH. The temperature that an enzyme works fastest at is called its _____ temperature. High temperatures and changes in pH _____ the enzyme, changing the shape of the _____ site. This means that the _____ can no longer bind to the enzyme. Different enzymes work best at different temperatures and pH levels.

B3.6 How the digestive system works

A Digestive enzymes act on specific food molecules. The enzymes help to break the large, insoluble molecules down into small, soluble molecules. These can then pass into the bloodstream.

The list below shows organs in the digestive system.

Tick the boxes for any organs where digestive enzymes are produced.

W gullet ☐

X stomach ☐

Y pancreas ☐

Z small intestine ☐

B Draw a line to match each food molecule to the enzyme that helps to break it down.

Food molecule
protein
lipid
starch

Enzyme
amylase
protease
lipase

C Circle **true** or **false** for each statement. Use the graph opposite to help you.

a The optimum pH of pancreatic amylase is around 8. **true/false**

b Pancreatic amylase does not work at pHs below 4. **true/false**

c Pancreatic amylase works best in acidic solutions. **true/false**

d pH affects the rate of a reaction catalysed by pancreatic amylase. **true/false**

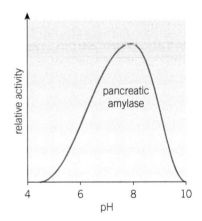

What you need to remember

Digestive enzymes are produced by specialised cells in _____ and in the lining of the digestive system. The enzymes are released from the cells into the digestive system where they mix with food. The enzymes catalyse the breakdown of large, _____ food molecules into smaller, soluble molecules that can be absorbed into the bloodstream. _____ such as amylase catalyse the breakdown of carbohydrates to simple sugars. Proteases catalyse the breakdown of _____ to amino acids. _____ catalyse the breakdown of _____ to fatty acids and glycerol.

B3.7 Making digestion efficient

A A student investigated the effect of acid on pepsin (the protease found in the stomach).

1. They set up three test tubes with: pepsin; hydrochloric acid; and pepsin and acid.
2. They measured the mass of three pieces of cooked egg white.
3. They placed one piece into each test tube and left them for 1 hour in a water bath at 37 °C.
4. Finally, they removed the pieces of egg white, dried them, and measured their mass.

The results are shown below.

Solution in the test tube	Mass of egg white at start in g	Mass of egg white at end in g	Mass loss in g
pepsin only	1.3	0.8	0.5
acid only	1.4	1.2	0.2
pepsin and acid	1.5	0.5	

a Calculate the missing result.

b Describe what the results show.

_____

_____

B The liver produces bile, which is stored in the gall bladder.

Which of these is a function of bile?

Tick **two** boxes.

W Contains enzymes to help break down food. ☐

X Neutralises the acidic liquid that comes from the stomach. ☐

Y Breaks down large fat droplets to increase their surface area. ☐

Z Contains acid so protease enzymes work more effectively. ☐

What you need to remember

Protease enzymes in the stomach work best in acidic conditions. The stomach produces hydrochloric

_____, which maintains a _____ pH. The enzymes made in the pancreas and the

small intestine work best in _____ conditions. Bile is produced by the _____ and

stored in the _____. It is released along the bile _____ into the duodenum. It has an

alkaline pH to _____ stomach acid. Bile also breaks down large fat globules into _____

droplets. This is called emulsifying.

B3 Practice questions

01 A student investigated the effect of pH on the rate of the reaction catalysed by amylase.

This is the method they followed:

1. Place a test tube containing 15 cm³ of starch solution in a water bath at 37 °C.
2. Add an acidic solution to the starch solution to give a pH of 4.
3. Set up a spotting tile with a drop of iodine in each well.
4. Mix 5 cm³ of amylase into the starch solution and start a stop-clock.
5. Take samples every 10 seconds using a pipette and add to an iodine-filled well.
6. Record the time taken for all the starch to be digested by the amylase.
7. Repeat for other pHs.

01.1 Describe what they would observe when the all the starch had been digested by the amylase. [1 mark]

HINT Amylase speeds up the breakdown of starch into simple sugars. Iodine turns blue-black when added to starch but stays orange when added to simple sugars.

_____

_____

01.2 Table 1 shows the results from the investigation.

Table 1

pH	Time taken for all the starch to be digested in seconds
4	150
5	150
6	60
7	40
8	60
9	70

Describe what the student should do to check the reproducibility of their results. [2 marks]

_____

_____

_____

_____

01.3 Complete the graph in **Figure 1** by:

● labelling the y-axis
● plotting the points from the table
● drawing a line of best fit. [4 marks]

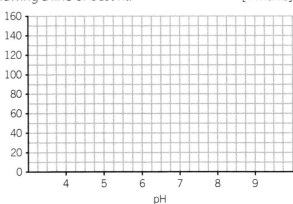

Figure 1

01.4 Describe what the results from the investigation show about the effect of pH on the rate of the reaction catalysed by amylase. [2 marks]

_____

_____

_____

_____

02 Use the words below to label **Figure 2**.

liver　　　　**pancreas**　　　　**gall bladder**

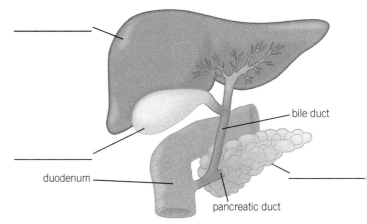

Figure 2

[3 marks]

B3 Checklist

	Student Book	☺	☺	☹
I can describe how specialised cells become organised into tissues.	3.1			
I can describe how several different tissues work together to form an organ.	3.1			
I can identify the main organs of the human digestive system.	3.2			
I can describe the basic structures of carbohydrates, proteins, and lipids.	3.3			
I can define what a catalyst is.	3.4			
I can describe enzymes as biological catalysts.	3.4			
I can describe what the metabolism of the body involves.	3.4			
I can explain how temperature and pH affect enzyme action.	3.5			
I can describe enzymes as working fastest at different temperatures and pH values.	3.5			
I can describe how the food I eat is digested in my body.	3.6			
I can describe the roles played by the different digestive enzymes.	3.6			
I can describe how hydrochloric acid and bile make digestion more efficient.	3.7			

B4.1 The blood

A Your blood is a tissue made up of several parts.

Draw a line to match each part of the blood to its function.

Part of the blood	Function
plasma	form part of the body's defence system against harmful microorganisms
red blood cells	pick up oxygen from the lungs and carry it to all the body cells
white blood cells	transports all of the blood cells and other substances around the body
platelets	help the blood to clot at the site of a wound

B The diagram below is based on an image of blood seen under a microscope.

Label the image using the names from activity **A** above.

C Red blood cells have adaptations that make them efficient at their job.

Draw a line to match each adaptation to its function.

Adaptation	Function
They contain the red pigment haemoglobin...	...giving them an increased surface area to volume ratio for diffusion.
They have no nucleus...	...to pick up oxygen.
They are biconcave discs (pushed in on both sides)...	...making more space for haemoglobin.
They are very flexible...	...to fit through narrow blood vessels.

What you need to remember

The blood, _____, and blood vessels make up the human circulatory system. _____ is a liquid that has blood cells suspended in it and transports other substances around the body. Red blood cells contain a red pigment called _____ that binds to oxygen to transport it from the _____ to body cells. White blood cells help to protect the body against infection with _____. Platelets are cell fragments that start the _____ process at wound sites.

B4.2 The blood vessels

A There are three main types of blood vessel: arteries, capillaries, and veins.

Label the diagrams with the name of each blood vessel.

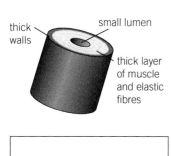

thick walls — small lumen — thick layer of muscle and elastic fibres

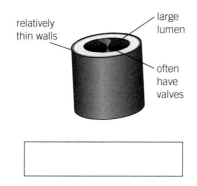

relatively thin walls — large lumen — often have valves

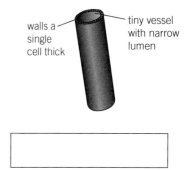

walls a single cell thick — tiny vessel with narrow lumen

B In humans and other mammals the blood vessels are arranged into a double circulatory system. You can see this in the diagram in activity **C** below.

What does a double circulatory system mean?

Tick the correct box.

Q It contains two types of blood vessel. ☐

R The heart has two chambers. ☐

S The blood travels to each place in the body twice. ☐

T The blood travels through the heart twice on each journey around the body. ☐

C The diagram opposite shows a double circulatory system.

Tick the boxes to show which type of blood vessel each letter is labelling.

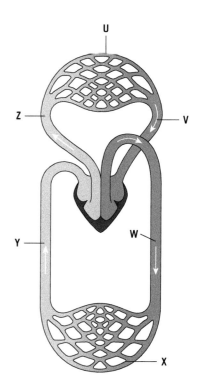

Letter	Artery	Vein	Capillaries
U			
V			
W			
X			
Y			
Z			

What you need to remember

Blood flows around the body in the blood vessels. The main types of blood vessel are arteries, _____, and capillaries. Substances diffuse in and out of the blood in the _____.

Veins have _____. These prevent backflow, ensuring that blood flows in the right direction.

_____ and other mammals have a _____ circulatory system. This contains two separate transport systems. One carries blood from the heart to the _____ to exchange gases. The other carries blood from the heart to all organs in the body and back again.

B4.3 The heart

A The function of the heart is to pump blood around the body.

a Circle the name of the blood vessel that brings oxygenated blood from the lungs to the heart.

b Draw a box around the name of the blood vessel that carries deoxygenated blood from the heart to the lungs.

c Underline the name of the blood vessel that brings deoxygenated blood to the heart.

d Draw a triangle around the name of the blood vessel that carries oxygenated blood away from the heart.

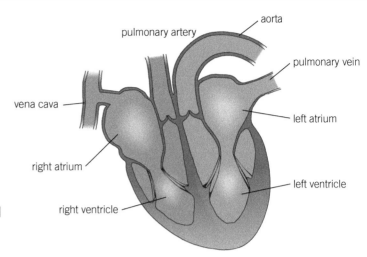

B Order the letters in the boxes below to show how blood passes through the heart.

The first one is done for you.

| U | | | | | |

P Blood is pushed into the arteries.

Q The atria contract.

R Blood is pushed into the right and left ventricles.

S Blood enters the right and left atria.

T The ventricles contract.

U Blood is in veins.

C Use the words below to fill in the gaps in this information about problems with the heart.

bypass   **oxygen**   **stent**   **heart**   **fatty**   **attack**   **statins**

The coronary arteries supply blood to the _____ muscle. In coronary heart disease they become narrow, usually because of _____ material building up inside.

This reduces the supply of _____ to the heart muscle and can cause a heart _____ .

A _____ can be placed inside the blood vessel, holding it open.

In _____ surgery, narrow or blocked coronary arteries are replaced with bits of veins from other parts of the body.

_____ are drugs that reduce cholesterol levels in the blood and help reduce fatty material building up.

What you need to remember

It is an organ that pumps _____ around the body. It contains _____ sides, each with chambers called an atrium and a _____ . The right side pumps blood to the _____ . The _____ side pumps blood all around the body. Heart _____ keep the blood flowing in the right direction.

Coronary heart disease is caused by narrow or blocked arteries that supply the heart muscle with _____ . Treatments include _____ , bypass surgery, and drugs called _____ .

B4.4 Helping the heart

A Which of these are treatments for a faulty heart valve?

Tick as many boxes as you need.

W artificial pacemaker ☐

X replacement mechanical valve ☐

Y heart transplant ☐

Z replacement valve from an animal ☐

B Read this information about heart transplants.

> When a person's heart fails completely they can have a heart transplant. The heart comes from a person who has died and donated their heart.
>
> The patient will have to wait for a donor heart that is a tissue match. As a result, many people die before they can have their transplant.
>
> Scientists have developed artificial, mechanical hearts that can be used whilst the patient waits for a heart transplant. These are expensive to make.

People have to wait for a heart transplant.

a Underline in red a social implication of this.

b Underline in blue an economic implication of using artificial hearts.

c There are ethical implications surrounding heart transplants. Underline in green a reason why.

C An artificial pacemaker is an electrical device used to correct an irregular heartbeat.

In 1993, there were about 121 300 operations to fit an artificial pacemaker in the USA. By 2009, that number was 188 700.

a Calculate the rise in the number of artificial pacemaker operations.

_____

b Calculate this as a percentage rise. Give your answer to 1 decimal place.

_____

What you need to remember

Damaged heart valves can be replaced using biological or _____ valves. Biological valves are taken from _____ or human donors.

The resting heart rate of around 70 beats per minute is controlled by a group of cells in the right _____. This is called the _____.

_____ pacemakers are electrical devices used to correct irregularities in the heart rhythm.

If a person's heart fails they can have a transplant. _____ hearts are occasionally used to keep patients alive while they wait for a transplant. They are also used to give a diseased heart a rest to help it recover.

B4.5 Breathing and gas exchange

A Use the words below to label the diagram of the human gas exchange system.

alveoli   bronchi   bronchiole   lungs   trachea

B What happens during breathing in?

Tick as many boxes as you need.

W ribs move up and out   ☐

X diaphragm moves up   ☐

Y volume inside the chest cavity increases   ☐

Z pressure inside the chest cavity increases   ☐

C Exchange of gases between the air and the blood takes place in the alveoli. This means that the percentage of some gases changes between the air you breathe in and the air you breathe out.

Circle the correct numbers in the table below.

Gas	% in air breathed in	% in air breathed out
carbon dioxide	0.04/4	0.04/4
nitrogen	20/80	20/80
oxygen	16/20	16/20

What you need to remember

The lungs are in your chest cavity, protected by your _____ and separated from your abdomen by a sheet of muscle called the _____ . During breathing in, air travels down the _____ and into smaller and smaller tubes that end in air sacs called alveoli. The alveoli provide a very large surface _____ and a rich supply of blood _____ . This means gases can diffuse into and out of the blood as efficiently as possible. During gas exchange, _____ passes from the alveoli into the blood and carbon dioxide passes from the _____ into the alveoli.

B4.6 Tissues and organs in plants

A Four main plant organs are labelled **S–V** on the diagram.

Draw lines to match each label to the name of the organ, and then to its function.

Letter	Organ	Function
S	leaf	supports the leaves and flowers
T	roots	where photosynthesis is carried out
U	stem	used for reproduction
V	flower	take up water and mineral ions

B Use the words below to label the diagram of a leaf cross-section.

vascular bundle

stomata

upper epidermis

palisade mesophyll

guard cell

air space

spongy mesophyll

lower epidermis

C Which plant organs are part of the plant's transport system?

Tick as many boxes as you need.

W flower ☐   **Y** stem ☐

X leaf ☐   **Z** root ☐

What you need to remember

Plant organs include the flowers, stem, leaves, and _____ . They are made up of several different tissues. The function of the leaf is to carry out _____ . One example of a tissue in the leaf is the lower _____ . It contains holes called _____ , which allow gases to enter and leave the leaf. The roots, _____ , and leaves form a plant organ system for the transport of substances around the plant.

B4.7 Transport systems in plants

A Tick the correct boxes to show how water, mineral ions, and sugars are moved around the plant.

Substance	✓ if carried in the xylem	✓ if carried in the phloem	✓ if moved from roots to leaves	✓ if moved from leaves to the rest of the plant
water				
mineral ions				
sugars				

B What is the movement of dissolved sugars around a plant called?

Tick **one** box.

W photosynthesis ☐

X transpiration ☐

Y translocation ☐

Z osmosis ☐

C The transport systems in a plant are vital to their survival.

Circle **true** or **false** for each statement.

a The plant makes sugar during photosynthesis. **true/false**

b Plant cells need sugars for respiration. **true/false**

c Water moves from the leaves down to the roots. **true/false**

d Plants need water for support. **true/false**

e Water is made during photosynthesis. **true/false**

What you need to remember

Plants have separate transport systems.

_____ tissue transports water and mineral ions from the _____ to the stems and leaves. Sugar is made in the _____ during photosynthesis. _____ tissue transports dissolved sugars from the leaves to the rest of the plant, including the growing regions and storage organs.

Plants need sugars to release _____ via respiration. They also use them for growth. Mineral ions are used to make _____ . Water is needed for photosynthesis as well as keeping the cells rigid so the plant is supported.

B4.8 Evaporation and transpiration

A Plants need to exchange gases with the air for photosynthesis.

Tick the boxes in the table opposite to show the direction of net diffusion of gases in and out of the leaf.

Substance	✓ if diffused into the leaf	✓ if diffused out of the leaf
water vapour		
oxygen		
carbon dioxide		

B Water moves in one direction through a plant.

Order the statements to show how this happens. Write the letters in the boxes to show the correct order. Use the diagram opposite to help you.

P Water moves from the roots into the stem.

Q Water moves into the roots by osmosis.

R Water evaporates into the air through the stomata.

S Water moves into the leaves.

T Water moves up through the stem.

C A student views the underside of a leaf using a microscope. The image opposite shows what they see.

The area of the field of view is 0.05 mm².

Estimate how many stomata would be found in:

a an area of 1 mm²

_____

b the whole underside of the leaf (area of 70 mm²).

_____

What you need to remember

The loss of water vapour from the surface of plant leaves is known as _____ . Water is lost through tiny holes in the underside of the _____ called stomata. The _____ cells control their opening and closing.

Stomata open to let _____ in for photosynthesis. At the same time, _____ vapour can evaporate from the leaves. This causes more water to be pulled up through the _____ tubes to take its place.

B4.9 Factors affecting transpiration

A Which of these conditions will result in a fast rate of transpiration?

Tick as many boxes as you need.

R	hot	☐	**U**	windy	☐
S	wet	☐	**V**	humid	☐
T	dry	☐	**W**	dark	☐

B The equipment opposite is used to measure the rate of transpiration.

What is it called?

Tick the correct box.

X barometer ☐

Y potometer ☐

Z burette ☐

leafy shoot — water — reservoir — air bubble — capillary tube filled with water — scale

C A student used the equipment in activity **B** above to study the effect of different factors on the rate of transpiration.

They drew a graph of their results.

Give **two** conclusions that can be drawn from the graph.

1 _____

_____

_____

2 _____

_____

rate of transpiration in mm³/min — light intensity in lux — X = windy, Y = still air

---

What you need to remember

Factors that _____ the rate of photosynthesis will increase the rate of transpiration. This is because more stomata will be open to let _____ into the leaf. When stomata are open, _____ _____ is lost by evaporation. Therefore, an increase in _____ intensity will increase the rate of transpiration.

Also, factors that affect the evaporation rate will affect the rate of transpiration. These factors include _____ , humidity, and air flow. The rate of transpiration can be measured using equipment called a _____ . Transpiration is _____ in hot, dry, windy, or bright conditions.

B4 Practice questions

01 Blood is a tissue consisting of a liquid called plasma, in which cells and platelets are suspended.

01.1 Describe the function of red blood cells. [2 marks]

_____

_____

_____

_____

01.2 **Figure 1** shows how much of each component is in a sample of blood.

plasma 55%

white blood cells and platelets <1%

red blood cells 45%

blood

Figure 1

The average person has 5 dm³ of blood.

Use the data in **Figure 1** to calculate the volume of blood that is red blood cells. [2 marks]

HINT The percentage of a total = total × $\left(\dfrac{\text{percentage}}{100}\right)$.

_____ dm³

02 **Figure 2** shows a cross-section of a blood vessel. It is based on an image taken using a light microscope.

red blood cell

wall of blood vessel

lumen of blood vessel

1 µm

Figure 2

02.1 What type of blood vessel is shown in **Figure 2**? [1 mark]

Tick **one** box.

HINT Arteries and veins are large blood vessels. Capillaries are microscopic blood vessels.

X artery ☐

Y capillary ☐

Z vein ☐

02.2 Explain how you decided on your answer to **02.1**. [1 mark]

_____

_____

_____

02.3 A scientist used a light microscope to measure the rate of flow of red blood cells through the blood vessel.

They observed that a red blood cell travelled 1 mm in 1.4 seconds.

Calculate the rate of flow of the red blood cell. Include the correct unit. [4 marks]

_____

B4 Checklist

	Student Book	☺	☺	☹
I can describe how substances are transported to and from cells.	4.1			
I can identify the different components in the blood.	4.1			
I can give the functions of each main component of the blood.	4.1			
I can describe how the blood flows around the body.	4.2			
I can name the different types of blood vessel.	4.2			
I can describe why valves are important.	4.2			
I can explain the importance of a double circulatory system.	4.2			
I can describe the structure and functions of the heart.	4.3			
I can describe ways of solving problems with the blood supply to the heart and problems with valves.	4.3			
I can describe how the heart keeps its natural rhythm.	4.4			
I can explain how artificial pacemakers work.	4.4			
I can describe what artificial hearts can do.	4.4			
I can identify parts of the human gas exchange system.	4.5			
I can describe how gases are exchanged in the alveoli of the lungs.	4.5			
I can describe the roles of organs in the plant organ system for the transport of substances around the plant.	4.6			
I can name the substances that are transported in plants.	4.7			
I can describe how transport in the xylem tissue differs from transport in the phloem tissue.	4.7			
I can describe what transpiration is.	4.8			
I can describe the role of stomata and guard cells in controlling gas exchange and water loss.	4.8			
I can name the factors that affect the rate of transpiration.	4.9			
I can suggest ways of investigating the effect of environmental factors on rates of water uptake in the plant.	4.9			

B5.1 Health and disease

A Diseases can be communicable (infectious) or non-communicable.

Circle the communicable diseases in the list below.

heart disease   **measles**   **type 2 diabetes**   **depression**   **tuberculosis**

B Draw a line to match each factor to the disease it can cause.

Factor		Disease
stress		obesity
diet		lung cancer
smoking		depression
poor water quality		diarrhoea-linked diseases

C A group of scientists investigated a hypothesis: 'The more children a person has, the more likely the person is to suffer from stress.'

They collected data from 100 adults. They asked them how many children they had and how stressed they felt on an average day, as a score out of 10.

Draw a line on the graph axis below to show the trend in data they should see if their hypothesis is correct.

stress score

number of children

What you need to remember

Health is a state of physical and _____ well-being. Diseases are major causes of ill-health. Some are communicable. This means they are _____ and can pass from person to person. They are caused by _____ , for example, bacteria and viruses. Other diseases are _____ . An example is arthritis. Other factors, including food eaten (_____), stress, and life situations may have an effect on both mental and physical health. Different types of disease may and often do interact.

B5.2 Pathogens and disease

A Communicable diseases are caused by microorganisms.

Circle **true** or **false** for the following statements about microorganisms.

a Microorganisms that cause disease are called pathogens.   **true/false**

b Plants cannot be infected by microorganisms.   **true/false**

c All types of bacteria cause disease.   **true/false**

d Viruses are smaller than bacteria.   **true/false**

B Viruses cause disease by destroying cells.
The diagrams opposite show how they do this.
However, the diagrams are in the wrong order.

Write the letters in the boxes below to show the
correct order.

P

The viral genes cause the host
cell to make new viruses.

Q

The genetic material from the
virus is injected into the host cell.

R

The virus attaches to
a specific host cell.

S

The host cell splits open,
releasing the new viruses.

C Use the words below to complete the description of how bacteria cause disease.

headache	**cells**	**divide**	**toxins**	**fission**

Once bacteria enter your body they _____ rapidly by splitting in two. The process is called

_____ .

They may produce _____ (poisons) that affect your body and make you feel ill. Sometimes they directly

damage your _____ .

Signs that you have a bacterial infection could be a high temperature, a _____ , or a rash. These are

caused by your body responding to the cell damage and the poisons.

D Draw a line to match each disease to the way it is spread.

Disease

common cold

cholera

chlamydia

Spread by...

direct contact

air

water

What you need to remember

Communicable diseases are caused by _____ called pathogens, which include bacteria,
_____ , fungi, and protists. Bacteria and viruses reproduce rapidly inside your body. Bacteria can
damage cells or produce _____ that make you feel ill. _____ live and reproduce inside
your cells, causing cell damage. Pathogens can be spread by direct contact, by _____ , or by water.

B5.3 Preventing infections

A Ignaz Semmelweis was a scientist in the mid-1850s. He worked in a hospital where women had their babies. He carried out an important investigation into the cause of infectious diseases.

Draw a line to match each stage of a scientific investigation to the findings of Semmelweis.

Stage	Finding
observation	Make doctors wash their hands.
hypothesis	The pregnant women delivered by doctors rather than midwives were much more likely to die of a fever.
method	The number of deaths decreased.
results	Doctors are carrying the cause of disease on their hands.
conclusion	The hypothesis is correct, but the infectious agent is not known.

B We now know that the infectious agent described in activity **A** was a microorganism. What equipment helped scientists to work this out?

Tick the correct box.

R telescope ☐   **T** microscope ☐

S Bunsen burner ☐   **U** potometer ☐

C There are many ways of preventing the spread of a communicable disease:

V coughing/sneezing into a tissue

W keeping raw meat away from salad

X isolating infected people

Y destroying vectors (organisms that carry the pathogen)

Z vaccination

For each disease, write in the letter that represents the best method to prevent it.

malaria ☐

measles ☐

common cold ☐

Salmonella (food poisoning) ☐

Ebola ☐

What you need to remember

The work of many different scientists helped prove that communicable diseases are caused by _____.
The _____ of disease can be prevented in many ways.

Simple hygiene measures include hand _____, sneezing into a tissue, using disinfectants, destroying _____ that carry the pathogen, isolating infected individuals, and vaccination.

B5.4 Viral diseases

A Some communicable diseases are caused by viruses.

Write a letter and a number next to each disease to show its main symptoms and how the disease is spread.

Main symptoms

T	many infections or certain cancers

U	pattern of discoloration on the leaves

V	fever and red skin rash

How it is spread

1	droplets in the air

2	exchange of body fluids

3	direct contact and insect vectors

measles _____   HIV/AIDS _____   tobacco mosaic virus _____

B The graph below shows the number of people infected with measles in the UK from 1940 to 2005.

What conclusions can be drawn from the graph? Tick the correct boxes.

W Infection with measles was rare in 2005. ☐

X Measles is a disease that can kill. ☐

Y Vaccination helped decrease the number of measles infections. ☐

Z The largest epidemic of measles happened in the early 1960s. ☐

C Circle **true** or **false** for the following statements about HIV/AIDS.

a HIV is a virus. **true/false**

b Only drug users that share needles can get HIV. **true/false**

c HIV attacks cells in the immune system. **true/false**

d AIDS develops when a person can no longer fight off infections. **true/false**

What you need to remember

The _____ virus is spread by drops in the air. It causes fever and a rash, and can kill. There is no cure but there is a _____ , which has reduced the number of cases in the UK.

HIV attacks the body's _____ cells. It can be treated with antiviral drugs. If it is not treated then _____ occurs. This means that the body's immune system has become so badly damaged it can no longer deal with other infections or cancers. HIV is spread by the exchange of body fluids, such as _____ or breast milk.

Tobacco _____ virus (TMV) is spread by contact and insect _____ . It damages leaves and reduces _____ so the plant can no longer make its own food. There is no treatment. Spread is prevented by field hygiene and pest control.

B5.5 Bacterial diseases

A Some communicable diseases are caused by bacteria.

Draw a line to match each bacterial disease to the main symptoms it causes.

Bacterial disease		Main symptoms
Salmonella		discharge from vagina or penis
gonorrhoea		vomiting and diarrhoea
Agrobacterium tumefaciens infection		mass of cells on the shoot (crown gall)

B *Salmonella* is a type of bacteria that causes food poisoning. It is found in raw meat, usually chicken.

Circle the correct **bold** words in the bullet points below to complete advice on how to prevent being infected with *Salmonella*.

- Keep **raw/cooked** chicken away from food that is eaten uncooked, such as salads.

- Store raw chicken in a **fridge/warm kitchen**.

- **Always/do not** wash raw chicken.

- Wash hands and surfaces **before/after** handling raw chicken.

- Make sure the **outside only/whole chicken** is cooked thoroughly.

C Why is it difficult to treat gonorrhoea with antibiotics?

Tick the correct box.

X It is not caused by bacteria. ☐

Y Strains have evolved that are resistant to many antibiotics. ☐

Z It is a sexually transmitted disease. ☐

What you need to remember

Salmonella is a _____ spread through undercooked food. Symptoms include diarrhoea and vomiting caused by the _____ produced by the bacteria. In the UK, poultry are _____ against *Salmonella* to control the spread of disease.

Gonorrhoea is an STD (_____ transmitted disease). Symptoms include discharge from the _____ or vagina, and pain on urination. Treatment involves using _____, although many strains are now resistant. Using a barrier method of contraception (such as _____) and limiting the number of sexual partners prevents spread.

There are relatively few bacterial diseases of _____ but *Agrobacterium tumefaciens* causes crown galls. A crown gall is a mass of unspecialised _____ that grows on the shoots.

B5.6 Diseases caused by fungi and protists

A Diseases may be caused by fungi or protists.

a Circle the diseases that are caused by fungi.

b Underline the diseases that are caused by protists.

One disease is caused by neither (it is a bacterial infection).

malaria   **rose black spot**   **athlete's foot**   **tuberculosis**   **stem rust**

B A rose becomes infected with black spot. It has black spots on its leaves. If it is not treated it will die.

Tick the box that explains why.

W It will not be able to take up water.   ☐

X It will not be able to make enough food.   ☐

Y It will not flower well.   ☐

Z Its stems will weaken.   ☐

C Malaria is caused by protists. They are carried inside mosquitoes. There are different methods used to control the spread of malaria.

Draw a line to match the start of each sentence to its end.

Insecticides are used in homes and offices to...	...prevent mosquitoes biting people at night.
Insect nets over beds...	...kill the protists in the blood.
Antimalarial drugs...	...kill adult mosquitoes.
Areas of standing water are drained to...	...remove mosquito larvae.

What you need to remember

Rose black spot is a disease caused by _____. It is spread by wind and water. It damages leaves so they drop off. This affects growth as _____ is reduced. The spread of the disease is controlled by removing affected leaves and using chemical sprays.

_____ is caused by protists and is spread by the bite of female mosquitoes. It damages blood and _____ cells, causes fevers and shaking, and can be fatal. The spread of malaria is reduced by preventing mosquitoes from breeding, using mosquito _____ to prevent people from being bitten, and using drugs to kill the parasites in the _____ if a person gets bitten.

B5.7 Human defence responses

A Circle the organs that defend the body against pathogens.

heart   stomach   skin   liver   nose   mouth

B There are three main ways in which your white blood cells destroy pathogens.

Draw a line to match each role to the correct diagram.

Role	Diagram
producing antibodies	
producing antitoxins	
ingesting pathogens	

C Tick the box for each statement about antibodies that is correct.

W They are living organisms. ☐
X They are produced by white blood cells. ☐
Y They bind to the toxins that bacteria produce. ☐
Z They are specific – each antibody attacks one type of pathogen. ☐

What you need to remember

Your body has several lines of defence against the entry of pathogens. The skin is a _____. If you get cut, _____ in your blood start a clot to form. This dries into a scab, sealing the cut. The skin also produces antimicrobial secretions that destroy pathogens.

Pathogens can enter the body through the respiratory system. The nose, _____, and bronchi produce sticky _____ to trap pathogens. Tiny hairs called _____ sweep the mucus up to the back of the throat where it is swallowed and enters the stomach. The stomach produces strong _____, which kills the pathogens in the mucus. It also kills most of the pathogens you take in with _____ and drink.

Your white _____ cells help to defend you against pathogens by ingesting them and by making _____ and antitoxins.

B5 Practice questions

01 Pathogens cause communicable diseases in plants and animals.

01.1 Draw a line from each disease to the type of pathogen that causes it. [3 marks]

Disease	Pathogen
malaria	fungi
HIV/AIDS	bacteria
crown gall disease	virus
rose black spot	protist

01.2 Name the disease listed in **01.1** that is sexually transmitted. [1 mark]

HINT A sexually transmitted disease is also known as an STD.

_____

02 Cows can develop painful sores on the bottom of their hooves. These are caused by a bacterial infection.

Scientists carried out research into the best antibiotic cream to use to treat the sores.

02.1 Which definition best describes an antibiotic?
Tick **one** box. [1 mark]

W a chemical produced by white blood cells ☐

X a chemical that kills all living cells ☐

Y a drug that kills bacteria ☐

Z a substance that kills all microbes ☐

02.2 The scientists studied 183 different cows from three farms.

The cows were split into four groups and each group was given a different treatment. Three groups were treated with different antibiotics and one was treated with a cream that has no antibiotic properties.

The diameter of the sores on the cows' hooves was measured before treatment and then again after 30 days of treatment.

Name the variables used in this investigation. [2 marks]

Independent variable _____

_____

Dependent variable _____

_____

02.3 Explain why one group of cows was treated with a cream with no antibiotic properties. [2 marks]

_____

_____

_____

_____

02.4 The results are shown in **Table 1**.

Table 1

Treatment	Mean diameter of sores before treatment in cm	Mean diameter of sores after 30 days of treatment in cm
antibiotic **A**	2.01	1.11
antibiotic **B**	1.95	0.45
antibiotic **C**	2.14	1.29
cream with no antibiotic properties	1.96	2.25

A farmer wants to know which antibiotic to use to treat sores on his cows.

Explain which you would recommend and why. [3 marks]

_____

_____

_____

_____

B5 Checklist

	Student Book	☺	😐	☹
I can define what health is.	5.1			
I can suggest the different causes of ill health.	5.1			
I can describe how different types of disease interact.	5.1			
I can define what pathogens are.	5.2			
I can describe how pathogens cause disease.	5.2			
I can explain the ways that pathogens are spread.	5.2			
I can describe how the spread of disease can be reduced or prevented.	5.3			
I can give examples of plant and animal diseases caused by viruses.	5.4			
I can give examples of plant and animal diseases caused by bacteria.	5.5			
I can give examples of animal diseases caused by fungi.	5.5			
I can give examples of animal diseases caused by protists.	5.6			
I can describe how the spread of diseases can be reduced or prevented.	5.6			
I can describe how my body stops pathogens getting in.	5.7			
I can explain how my white blood cells protect me from disease.	5.7			

B6.1 Vaccination

A Draw a line to match each term to its definition.

Term	Definition
vaccine	unique proteins on the surface of a cell
immune	contains dead or inactivated forms of a pathogen
antibody	a microorganism that causes disease
antigens	a protein made by white blood cells that binds to a specific pathogen
pathogen	protected against a disease because of the action of white blood cells

B A tetanus vaccination protects you from getting the disease.

Write the letters below in the boxes in the correct order to show how the vaccine works. Some have been done for you.

P White blood cells are stimulated to produce the correct antibodies.

Q The live tetanus bacteria are destroyed before they can multiply and make you ill.

R Antibodies attack and destroy the live bacteria.

S Memory white blood cells 'remember' the right antibody.

T A small amount of dead or inactive tetanus bacteria is introduced into your body.

U Live tetanus bacteria infect your body.

V White blood cells respond rapidly and make the right antibodies.

T		S				Q

Target level of childhood immunisation — % children immunised with MMR, years 1995–2007

C Which of the following conclusions can be made from the graphs opposite?

Tick as many boxes as you need.

W Not immunising enough children results in an increase in the number of measles cases a few years later. ☐

X If 90% of children are immunised against MMR then there will be no cases of measles. ☐

Y The number of children being immunised against MMR fell between 1995 and 2004. ☐

Z In 1995 the number of cases of measles was the highest it had ever been. ☐

number of measles cases in 100s, years 1996–2009

What you need to remember

Pathogens have unique proteins on their surface called _____. A _____ contains small amounts of dead or inactive forms of a pathogen. When it is injected into your body, your white blood cells produce _____. These attach to the antigens, destroying the pathogen.

If the same live pathogen re-enters the body, the _____ blood cells respond quickly to produce the correct antibodies, preventing infection.

If a large proportion of the population is immune to a pathogen, the spread of the pathogen is much reduced. This is called _____ immunity.

B6.2 Antibiotics and painkillers

A Below is a list of drugs.

a Underline the painkillers.

b Circle the antibiotics.

aspirin   **penicillin**   **paracetamol**   **nicotine**   **ibuprofen**

B Circle **true** or **false** for the following statements.

a Paracetamol makes you feel better by killing pathogens.   **true/false**

b Antiseptics kill bacteria.   **true/false**

c Antibiotics are used to kill bacteria and viruses.   **true/false**

d Antibiotics are becoming less useful.   **true/false**

C Painkillers, antiseptics, and antibiotics are all useful for treating medical problems. However, they have different uses.

Complete the table by ticking the columns to show which treatment should be used for each problem.

Problem	✓ if painkiller should be used	✓ if antiseptic should be used	✓ if antibiotic should be used
grazed knee			
migraine			
bacterial lung infection			
common cold			
sprained ankle			
bacterial blood infection			

D Some strains of bacteria have evolved so they are no longer killed by antibiotics.

What do we call this type of bacteria?

Tick **one** box.

W efficient ☐

X permanent ☐

Y persistent ☐

Z resistant ☐

What you need to remember

_____ such as aspirin treat the symptoms of disease, but do not kill the pathogens that cause it.

_____ cure bacterial diseases by killing the bacterial pathogens inside your body.

Strains of bacteria are evolving that are _____ to antibiotics. This is causing great concern.

Antibiotics do not destroy _____ because they reproduce inside _____. It is difficult to develop drugs that can destroy them without damaging your tissues.

B6.3 Discovering drugs

A There are a number of drugs used today that are based on traditional medicines extracted from plants and microorganisms.

Draw a line to match each drug to the organism it is extracted from.

Drug	Organism
aspirin	foxglove plant
digitalis	mould
penicillin	willow tree

B In 1928 Alexander Fleming was growing mould on his bacteria culture plates. He noticed a clear ring around some of the spots of mould.

What was his hypothesis based on this observation?

Tick **one** box.

W The mould is called *Penicillium*. ☐

X The mould had produced a substance that killed the bacteria. ☐

Y The bacteria slowed down the growth of the mould. ☐

Z The bacteria had produced a substance that killed the mould. ☐

C Scientists extract a chemical from a plant.

What do they need to do to see if it could be useful as a new antibiotic?

Circle **yes** or **no** for each statement.

a Test to see if it kills bacteria on culture plates. **yes/no**

b Test to see if it kills viruses. **yes/no**

c Test to see if it is safe to use on human cells. **yes/no**

d Test to see if it kills bacteria in infected animals. **yes/no**

What you need to remember

Traditionally drugs were extracted from _____ (e.g., digitalis from foxgloves) or from microorganisms (e.g., penicillin from _____). Penicillin is an _____ that was discovered by Alexander _____. Most new drugs are synthesised by chemists in the pharmaceutical industry. However, the starting point may still be a chemical extracted from a plant.

B6.4 Developing drugs

A There are many stages involved in developing a new drug.

Draw a line to match the start of each sentence to its end.

P	A low dose of the drug is given to healthy volunteers...

...to check if it treats the disease.

Q	The drug is tested on cells in the laboratory...

....to check it works in whole living organisms.

R	The drug is given to a small number of patients...

...to check for side effects.

S	The drug is tested on live animals...

...to check it is not toxic to living cells.

T	The drug is given to many patients...

...to find the optimum dose.

B Write the letters **P–T** from activity **A** above in the boxes below to show the correct order of the stages of drug development.

[ ] [ ] [ ] [ ] [ ]

C Choose from the words below to complete the paragraph about clinical trials.

doctor   **double-blind**   **effective**   **placebo**   **more**

controlled   **less**   **randomly**   **drug**

The patients are _____ placed into two groups. One group is given the drug and the other is given a _____ that does not contain the drug. Neither the _____ nor the patients know which they are getting. This is called a _____ trial.

The patients' health is monitored carefully. If the health of the patients who were given the drug improves _____ than those who had the placebo the scientists can be confident that the drug is _____ .

What you need to remember

New medical drugs are tested for many _____ before being used in patients. They must be effective, _____, stable, and successfully taken into and removed from the body.

New drugs are first tested in the laboratory using cells, tissues, and live _____. During clinical _____ the drug is tested on healthy volunteers and patients. Low doses are used to test for safety. Then larger numbers of patients take to drug to find the best _____. In double-_____ trials, some patients are given the drug and others are given a _____ that does not contain the drug. Neither the patient nor the _____ knows which they are receiving.

B6 Practice questions

01 Influenza (flu) is a communicable disease that can kill very young or elderly people.

01.1 A person who has flu cannot be treated with antibiotics.

Tick the **two** boxes that explain why. [2 marks]

HINT Remember, antibiotics are effective only against bacteria.

W Flu is caused by bacteria. ☐

X Flu is caused by a virus. ☐

Y Antibiotics only kill bacteria. ☐

Z Antibiotics only kill viruses. ☐

01.2 In the UK people over the age of 65 years are offered a free flu vaccination.

Explain how the vaccine prevents a person from getting flu. [4 marks]

HINT The flu vaccine contains dead viruses that the white blood cells attack.

_____

_____

_____

_____

_____

01.3 Scientists gathered the data shown in **Figure 1**.

Describe the trend in the percentage of people over 65 having the vaccination between 1990 and 2001. [1 mark]

HINT This graph has two y-axes and two sets of bars. Use the key to help you work out what the bars show.

_____

01.4 Calculate the number of people over 65 who received the flu vaccination in 2000–2001.

Show your working out and give your answer to 1 significant figure. [3 marks]

_____ people

01.5 Explain how a high percentage of people over 65 being vaccinated protects others who have not been vaccinated against flu. [2 marks]

HINT This is called herd immunity.

_____

_____

_____

_____

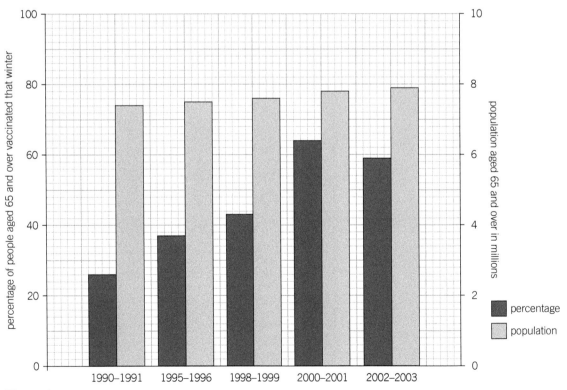

Figure 1

B6 Checklist

	Student Book	😊	😐	☹
I can describe how my immune system works.	6.1			
I can explain how vaccination protects me against disease.	6.1			
I can explain what medicines are and how some of them work.	6.2			
I can describe how painkillers and other medicines treat disease symptoms but do not kill pathogens.	6.2			
I can describe the ways in which antibiotics can and cannot be used.	6.2			
I can name some drugs traditionally extracted from plants.	6.3			
I can describe how penicillin was discovered.	6.3			
I can describe how scientists look for new drugs.	6.3			
I can name the stages involved in testing and trialling new drugs.	6.4			
I can explain why testing new drugs is important.	6.4			

B7.1 Non-communicable diseases

A There are many different risk factors for disease.

Draw a line to show if each risk factor is due to things you cannot change, lifestyle, or substances present in the environment.

your age •

lack of exercise •

UV light from the Sun •

radioactive substances in the air •

using sunbeds •

drinking alcohol •

your genes •

overeating •

| things you cannot change |

| lifestyle choices |

| effects of the environment |

B Gethyn has lung cancer. The list below shows some of the impacts of his disease.

P His treatments are making him feel very tired.

Q His treatments are paid for by the NHS.

R His friends and family have spent time looking after him and driving him to hospital appointments.

S He is unable to work.

a Which statement shows a personal impact of the disease? _____

b Which statement shows a social impact? _____

c Which **two** statements have economic impacts? _____ and _____

C 20 children aged 8–16 years were selected at random. The length of their feet was measured and they were asked to complete a mental arithmetic test. The scatter graph below shows the data collected.

Which of these statements is correct?
Tick **one** box.

W There is a correlation between foot length and ability to do mental arithmetic. ☐

X Having big feet makes you clever. ☐

Y There is a causal mechanism between foot length and ability to do mental arithmetic. ☐

Z Most of the children had big feet. ☐

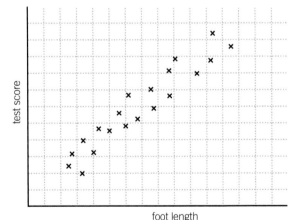

test score

foot length

What you need to remember

Non-communicable diseases cannot be _____ from one individual to another; they are not

infectious. _____ factors are aspects of a person's lifestyle, or substances present in a person's body

or environment, that have been shown to be linked to an _____ rate of a disease. A risk factor for

type 2 _____ is overeating.

For some non-communicable diseases, a _____ mechanism for some risk factors has been proven,

but not in others. For example, smoking causes _____ cancer because tar is a carcinogen.

B7.2 Cancer

A Label the diagram below with the words **tumour cells** and **normal cells**.

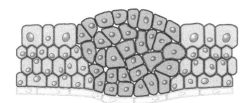

B For each statement in the table below, tick a box to show whether it is true for each type of tumour.

Some statements apply to both types.

Statement	✓ if true for benign tumours	✓ if true for malignant tumours
produced by uncontrolled cell division		
can be life-threatening		
spread around the body		
cells are contained in one place		
also known as cancer		
can form secondary tumours		

C Draw a line to match each type of cancer to the most probable cause.

Type of cancer	Cause
lung cancer	genetics
breast cancer	UV light
skin cancer	virus infection
cervical cancer	tar in tobacco smoke

What you need to remember

A tumour forms when there is abnormal, uncontrolled _____ division. _____
tumours form in one place and do not spread to other tissues. _____ tumour cells are cancers.
They invade neighbouring tissues and may spread to different parts of the body in the blood where they form
_____ tumours. They disrupt normal tissues and, if left untreated, may kill the person.

Lifestyle risk factors for cancer include smoking, obesity, viruses, and _____ light. There are also
genetic risk factors for some cancers. Cancer can be treated using _____ during radiotherapy or
_____ , which uses chemicals.

A Draw a line to match each health problem to the substance in tobacco smoke that causes it.

Health problem

shortage of oxygen in the blood ●

increase in heart rate ●

breakdown in alveoli ●

low birthweight ●

lung cancer ●

stillbirth ●

throat cancer ●

COPD ●

Substance

nicotine

carbon monoxide

tar

B What conclusions can be drawn from the graph opposite?

Tick the correct boxes.

W Smoking cigarettes increases your risk of developing lung cancer. ☐

X You can only get lung cancer from smoking cigarettes. ☐

Y The more cigarettes a person smokes per day, the higher their risk of lung cancer. ☐

Z If you smoke then you will get lung cancer. ☐

relative risk of lung cancer

80

70

60

50

40

30

20

10

0

0   1–10 11–20 21–30 31–30 40+

number of cigarettes smoked per day

C Circle the correct **bold** words in the text below to explain how smoking is linked to heart disease.

Scientists have data showing that men who smoke are more likely to die of heart disease than those who don't. This is a **correlation/causal mechanism**.

They have shown why this happens. This is a **correlation/causal mechanism**.

Nicotine/carbon monoxide makes the heart rate increase whilst other chemicals damage the lining of the arteries. This increases the risk of **clot formation/cholesterol**.

Chemicals in cigarette smoke also lead to **a decrease/an increase** in blood pressure.

What you need to remember

Tobacco smoke contains many substances including the addictive drug _____, the poisonous gas carbon _____ , and the carcinogen _____ .

Smoking can cause cardiovascular disease including coronary _____ disease, _____ cancer, and lung diseases such as _____ and COPD. If a pregnant woman smokes, her blood carries carbon monoxide, which restricts the amount of _____ the fetus gets. This can lead to premature birth, low _____ , and even stillbirth.

B7.4 Diet, exercise, and disease

A Overeating can lead to a person becoming obese.

Circle the health problems caused by obesity.

cervical cancer   **type 2 diabetes**   **COPD**   **heart disease**   **brain damage**

B People who exercise regularly are healthier than people who don't.

Match the start of each sentence to its end to explain why (the causal mechanisms).

Exercise increases muscle tissue...	...which reduces the risk of fatty deposits building up inside arteries.
Exercise lowers blood cholesterol levels...	...which lowers the risk of developing type 2 diabetes.
People who exercise are less likely to become obese...	...which increases metabolic rate.

C The graphs below show the effect of obesity on the risk of developing type 2 diabetes.

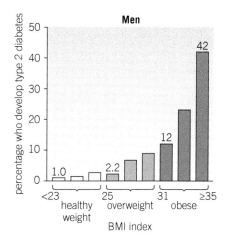 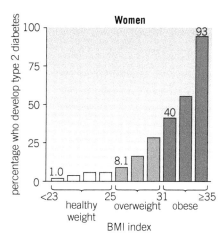

Describe **two** observations from the graphs.

1 _____

_____

2 _____

_____

What you need to remember

Eating more food than you need could make you _____. This can lead to serious health problems such as type 2 _____, high _____ pressure, and heart disease.

Regular _____ lowers blood cholesterol and reduces the risk of _____ deposits building up in the coronary arteries, lowering the risk of _____ disease.

B7.5 Alcohol and other carcinogens

A Drinking alcohol has several effects on the body.

Write these effects in the correct box on the diagram opposite:

unconsciousness

feeling relaxed and happy

difficulty walking and talking

death

no alcohol

INCREASING INTAKE

How a person would be affected

excessive alcohol

B Tick the boxes to show which organs alcohol can damage.

W pancreas ☐

X liver ☐

Y brain ☐

Z intestines ☐

C Carcinogens are risk factors for cancer. Ionising radiation and some chemicals can be carcinogens.

Draw a line from each carcinogen to show if it is a chemical or ionising radiation.

Carcinogen

chemical		ionising radiation
	tar (from smoking)	
	UV light	
	X-rays	
	alcohol	
	radon gas	

What you need to remember

Alcohol is an addictive drug that affects the _____ system. A small amount makes people feel

relaxed and _____ down their reactions. Drinking a large dose can lead to unconsciousness,

_____ , and even death. Long-term use can cause cirrhosis, _____ cancer, and brain

damage. Alcohol taken in by a _____ woman can affect the development of her unborn baby.

Ionising radiation is a risk factor for cancer because it causes _____ in the DNA. An example is

ultraviolet (UV) light from the _____ , which increases the risk of _____ cancers.

B7 Practice questions

01 Mouth cancer results if a tumour develops on the surface of the tongue, mouth, lips, or gums.

It is a non-communicable disease.

Define these terms:

HINT Communicable also means infectious.

01.1 tumour [2 marks]

_____

_____

_____

01.2 non-communicable disease [1 mark]

_____

_____

_____

02 **Figure 1** shows the effects of smoking and drinking alcohol on the risk of developing mouth cancer.

Figure 1

02.1 Which conclusions are correct?

Tick **two** boxes. [2 marks]

W If you do not smoke you will not get mouth cancer. ☐

X If a person drinks less alcohol it will decrease their risk of developing mouth cancer. ☐

Y Both smoking and drinking alcohol are risk factors for mouth cancer. ☐

Z Smoking and drinking alcohol are the only risk factors for mouth cancer. ☐

02.2 A doctor carries out a survey on some of her patients.

During an interview she asks five patients how many cigarettes they smoke per day and how much alcohol they drink, on average.

The information is shown in **Table 1**.

Table 1

Patient	Average number of cigarettes smoked per day	Average number of alcoholic drinks per day
A	22	2
B	0	5
C	45	4
D	0	1
E	30	6

Explain why this information may not be accurate. [1 mark]

_____

_____

_____

02.3 Write the letters from **Table 1** in the boxes below to order the patients' risk of developing mouth cancer.

Use the data in **Figure 1**. [2 marks]

low risk   high risk

☐   ☐   ☐   ☐   ☐

02.4 Other than cancer, name **one** non-communicable disease that smoking is a risk factor for. [1 mark]

HINT The smoke and tar from smoking affect the lungs. Nicotine raises blood pressure.

_____

B7 Checklist

	Student Book	☺	☺	☹
I can define non-communicable disease.	7.1			
I can define lifestyle factor.	7.1			
I can describe how scientists consider risk.	7.1			
I can describe the human and financial costs involved in non-communicable diseases.	7.1			
I can define causal mechanism.	7.1			
I can describe what a tumour is.	7.2			
I can explain the difference between benign and malignant tumours.	7.2			
I can describe how cancer spreads.	7.2			
I can explain how smoking affects the risk of developing cardiovascular disease.	7.3			
I can explain how smoking affects the risk of developing lung disease and lung cancer.	7.3			
I can describe the effect of smoking on unborn babies.	7.3			
I can describe the effect of diet and exercise on the development of obesity.	7.4			
I can describe how diet and exercise affect the risk of developing cardiovascular disease.	7.4			
I can describe obesity as a risk factor for type 2 diabetes.	7.4			
I can describe alcohol as a factor that affects liver and brain function.	7.5			
I can describe alcohol as a factor that can affect unborn babies.	7.5			
I can describe alcohol as a carcinogen.	7.5			
I can name other agents that act as carcinogens.	7.5			

B8.1 Photosynthesis

A Use the words and formulae below to complete the word and symbol equations for photosynthesis.

$C_6H_{12}O_6$ oxygen   light CO_2 water

carbon dioxide   + _____ $\xrightarrow{\hspace{2cm}}$ glucose   + _____

6 _____ + $6H_2O$ $\xrightarrow{\hspace{2cm}}$ _____ $+ 6O_2$

B A student carried out an experiment using the equipment shown opposite.

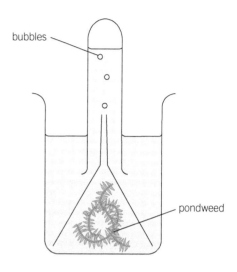
bubbles

pondweed

She placed pondweed in some water and shone a lamp on it. She observed bubbles collecting in the test tube.

She placed a glowing splint into the test tube and it relit.

a Underline the section of text that is evidence that a plant makes a gas during photosynthesis.

b Circle the section of text that is evidence that the gas is oxygen.

C The leaves of a plant are adapted to carry out photosynthesis.

Draw a line to match each adaptation to its function.

Adaptation of leaf	Function
broad shape	to allow carbon dioxide to enter the leaf and oxygen to leave
thin	to bring water to the cells
stomata	big surface area for light to fall on
veins	allow carbon dioxide to get to cells and oxygen to leave, by diffusion
air spaces	diffusion distances for gases are short

What you need to remember

Photosynthesis is an _____ reaction that takes place in the cells in _____ and plant leaves. Energy is transferred from the environment to the chloroplast by _____ . It is used to convert carbon dioxide and _____ into sugar (glucose).

A green substance called _____ captures the light.

Photosynthesis can be summarised as follows: carbon dioxide + water → _____ + oxygen.

Leaves are well adapted to allow the maximum amount of photosynthesis to take place.

B8.2 The rate of photosynthesis

A You can investigate the effect of light intensity on the rate of photosynthesis.

Draw a line from each variable in the investigation to its type.

Variable

temperature of water ●

distance from light to plant ●

type of plant ●

volume of oxygen produced after 5 minutes ●

temperature of room ●

concentration of carbon dioxide in the water ●

Type

| independent variable |

| dependent variable |

| control variable |

B Which of the graphs below correctly shows the results obtained from this investigation?

Tick the correct box.

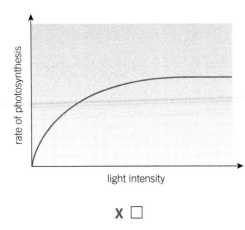

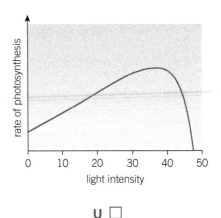

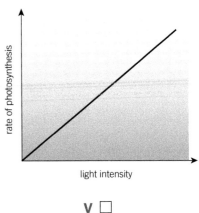

X ☐   **U** ☐   **V** ☐

C In certain conditions, the amount of photosynthesis a plant can carry out is limited. This is due to **limiting factors**.

Which of these are limiting factors for photosynthesis?

Tick the correct boxes.

W concentration of minerals in the soil ☐   **Y** temperature ☐

X carbon dioxide concentration ☐   **Z** amount of starch in leaves ☐

What you need to remember

The rate of photosynthesis may be affected by _____ intensity, temperature, concentration

of _____ _____ , and chlorophyll levels in the leaf. These are known as

_____ factors because at times any one or several of these things can be in short supply and limit

the rate.

For most plants the _____ the light, the faster the rate of photosynthesis. As temperature rises,

the rate of photosynthesis _____ up to a certain temperature. After this, _____ are

denatured and the rate falls. Increasing the concentration of carbon dioxide will _____ the rate

of photosynthesis.

B8.3 How plants use glucose

A You can test leaves for the presence of starch. The sentences below describe the stages in the method.

Draw a line to match the start of each sentence to its end.

1. Boil the leaf in ethanol to...	...test for starch.
2. Rinse the leaf in hot water to...	...remove the green colour.
3. Add iodine to the leaf to...	...soften the leaf.

B A student tested some plant parts for the presence of different food molecules.

Their results are shown below.

What was tested	Test		
	Added iodine	**Added to ethanol**	**Heated with Benedict's solution**
tuber (potato)	went black	stayed clear	went orange
seed (sunflower)	went black	went cloudy	stayed blue
fruit (apple)	stayed orange	stayed clear	went red

Which plant part(s) contains:

a sugars? _____

b starch? _____

c lipids? _____

C Circle **true** or **false** for the following statements.

a Plants carry out respiration 24 hours a day.   **true/false**

b Glucose is stored as starch because starch is soluble in water.   **true/false**

c Plants use glucose to make cellulose.   **true/false**

d Some plants can get nitrates from digesting animals.   **true/false**

e Only animals contain lipids (fats).   **true/false**

What you need to remember

Plant and algal cells use the glucose produced during photosynthesis for _____ to transfer energy.
They also convert the glucose into insoluble _____ for storage, and use it to produce fats or oils for
storage, _____ to strengthen cell walls, and amino acids.

Plants and algal cells also need _____ ions absorbed from the soil or water to make amino acids.
The amino acids are joined together to make _____ .

B8 Practice questions

01 A student carried out an investigation into how a limiting factor affects the rate of photosynthesis. The equipment they used is shown in **Figure 1**.

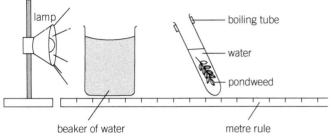

Figure 1

This is the method they used:

1. Place the pondweed 20 cm away from the lamp.
2. Leave the pondweed for 5 minutes.
3. Measure the pH of the water in the test tube.
4. Change the water in the test tube and repeat.
5. Repeat steps 1–5, moving the test tube away from the lamp by 20 cm each time.

01.1 Which limiting factor is the student investigating?

Tick **one** box. [1 mark]

W light intensity ☐

X carbon dioxide concentration ☐

Y temperature ☐

Z pH of water ☐

01.2 Use **Figure 1** to explain how the student is controlling the temperature of the pondweed.

[1 mark]

_____

_____

_____

01.3 Their results are shown in **Table 1**.

Table 1

Distance of lamp from pondweed in cm	pH of water around pondweed after 5 minutes		
	Trial 1	**Trial 2**	**Mean**
20	8.5	8.5	8.5
40	8.2	8.4	
60	7.7	7.9	7.8
80	7.6	7.5	7.55

Calculate the missing value in **Table 1**. [2 marks]

_____

01.4 If carbon dioxide is removed from water, the pH of the water becomes more alkaline (pH >7).

Explain what happened to the pH of the water after 5 minutes when the lamp was 20 cm away from the pondweed. [1 mark]

HINT Remember that '>' means 'more than'.

_____

_____

01.5 Explain why this happened. [2 marks]

_____

_____

_____

_____

_____

_____

01.6 Write a conclusion to explain the trend in the results. [3 marks]

HINT Your conclusion should describe the pattern (trend) in the results **and** explain why there is this trend. Make sure it contains three separate points (one for each mark).

_____

_____

_____

_____

_____

_____

_____

_____

_____

B8 Checklist

	Student Book	☺	☺	☹
I can name the raw materials and energy source for photosynthesis.	8.1			
I can describe photosynthesis as an endothermic reaction.	8.1			
I can write the equations that summarise photosynthesis.	8.1			
I can name the factors that limit the rate of photosynthesis in plants.	8.2			
I can describe how plants use the glucose they make.	8.3			
I can name the extra materials that plant cells need to produce proteins.	8.3			
I can describe some practical tests for starch, sugars, and proteins.	8.3			

B9.1 Aerobic respiration

A Aerobic respiration is a reaction that takes place in all living cells.

Draw a line from each substance to show if it is a reactant or a product of respiration.

Substance

reactant		carbon dioxide		product
		oxygen		
		water		
		glucose		

B Many of the stages of aerobic respiration take place in one part of the cell.

On the diagram of an animal cell below, label this part with its name.

C The energy transferred during respiration supplies all the energy needed for living processes in the cells.

Describe why the following cells need energy.

a a muscle cell

_____

_____

_____

_____

b a plant root hair cell

_____

_____

_____

_____

What you need to remember

Aerobic respiration is an _____ reaction that takes place in all living cells. It can be summarised as:

glucose + _____ → _____ _____ + water (+ energy transferred to the environment)

Most stages take place in the _____ of the cells. The _____ transferred is needed for living processes. Some organisms, such as humans, need it for keeping warm.

B9.2 The response to exercise

A Circle the correct **bold** words to complete the description of what happens when you exercise.

When you exercise your muscles start contracting **slower/faster**.

Your heart rate **decreases/increases** and the arteries supplying blood to your muscles **dilate/constrict**. This increases the flow of **deoxygenated/oxygenated** blood to the muscles.

Your breathing rate **decreases/increases** and you breathe more **shallowly/deeply**. This increases the amount of **oxygen/carbon dioxide** in the blood. It also allows **oxygen/carbon dioxide** to be removed more quickly from the blood.

B Name the carbohydrate used to store glucose in the muscles.

Tick the correct box.

W starch ☐

X insulin ☐

Y glucagon ☐

Z glycogen ☐

C Four Year 10 students measured their pulse rates at rest. They then ran on a treadmill at a speed of 8 km/h for 5 minutes and measured their pulse rates during the run. The results are shown below.

Student	Pulse rate in beats per minute	
	At rest	Maximum during exercise
Jasmine	80	145
Louise	72	142
Brandon	84	144
Ruby	65	139

Write the correct words in the gaps.

During exercise the pulse rates of all the students _____ .

Louise's pulse rate went up by _____ beats per minute.

_____ was the fittest person.

Her heart volume was probably the _____ .

What you need to remember

When you exercise your _____ help you move around. They need energy to contract.

During exercise the human body responds to the increased demand for energy. Body responses to exercise include:

- increases in the _____ rate, the breathing rate, and the breath volume
- _____ stores in the muscles are converted to glucose for respiration
- the flow of oxygenated _____ to the muscles increases.

These responses act to increase the rate of supply of glucose and _____ to the muscles.

They also increase the rate of removal of _____ _____ from the muscles.

B9.3 Anaerobic respiration

A Which of the following word equations correctly shows anaerobic respiration in animal cells?

Tick the correct box.

W glucose → lactic acid +carbon dioxide ☐

X glucose → lactic acid ☐

Y glucose → carbon dioxide + water ☐

Z glucose → carbon dioxide + ethanol ☐

B Tick the boxes to compare aerobic and anaerobic respiration in **animal** cells.

Some rows apply to both types of respiration.

	✓ if true for aerobic respiration	✓ if true for anaerobic respiration
Glucose is a reactant.		
Oxygen is a reactant.		
Carbon dioxide is produced.		
Energy is transferred to the environment.		
Cells can carry it out continuously.		

C Plants and microorganisms also carry out anaerobic respiration. These reactions can be useful for us.

Circle **true** or **false** for each statement.

a Anaerobic respiration in yeast is known as fermentation.   **true/false**

b The production of ethanol during bread-making makes the bread rise.   **true/false**

c Bacteria that produce lactic acid are used to make yoghurt.   **true/false**

d During the brewing process, yeast produces carbon dioxide.   **true/false**

What you need to remember

Anaerobic respiration is respiration without _____ . When this takes place in animal cells, glucose is incompletely broken down to form _____ acid. Because of this, anaerobic respiration transfers _____ energy than aerobic respiration.

When you exercise hard, your blood might not be able to supply the muscles with enough _____ so they use anaerobic respiration. The acid produced makes muscles tired.

Anaerobic respiration in _____ cells and some microorganisms, such as yeast, results in the production of _____ and carbon dioxide.

B9.4 Metabolism and the liver

A Which is the correct definition of metabolism?

Tick the correct box.

W the sum of all the chemical reactions in your body ☐

X how fast you transfer energy during respiration ☐

Y how easily you lose weight ☐

Z the amount of energy transferred from your body ☐

B Draw a line to match each word or symbol equation to the metabolic reaction it represents.

Equation	Metabolic reaction
$C_6H_{12}O_6 + 6O_2 \rightarrow 6H_2O + 6CO_2$	photosynthesis
sucrose $\rightarrow$ glucose + fructose	breakdown of molecules
$6H_2O + 6CO_2 \rightarrow C_6H_{12}O_6 + 6O_2$	respiration
amino acids $\rightarrow$ protein	formation of molecules

C Circle each correct word to describe a metabolic reaction.

The breakdown of excess	lipids	in the	stomach	to form	urea
	proteins		kidney		glucose
	sugars		liver		protein

What you need to remember

Metabolism is the sum of all the _____ in the body. The energy transferred by _____ in cells is used by the organism for the enzyme-controlled processes that synthesise new molecules or break molecules down.

Metabolism includes:

● the conversion of _____ to starch, glycogen, and cellulose

● the formation of lipid molecules

● the use of glucose and nitrate ions to form _____ acids, which are used to synthesise proteins

● the breakdown of excess proteins to form _____, which takes place in the _____.

01 Yeast is a single-celled fungus. It carries out anaerobic respiration.

01.1 Complete the word equation for this reaction. [1 mark]

> **HINT** Remember, energy is released during respiration but this is not a product, so it not included in the equation.

glucose →_____ + carbon dioxide

01.2 Give **one** reason why this reaction is useful to humans. [1 mark]

_____

01.3 Animals, such as humans, also carry out anaerobic respiration.

01.3.1 Give **one** way in which anaerobic respiration in animals and fungi is the same. [1 mark]

_____

01.3.2 Give **one** way in which anaerobic respiration in animals and fungi is different. [1 mark]

_____

02 A student was asked to carry out an investigation into the anaerobic respiration of yeast.

Figure 1 shows the equipment he was told to use.

The volume of carbon dioxide produced is measured using the syringe.

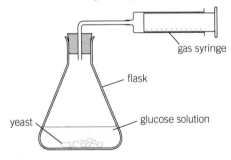

Figure 1

02.1 Explain how the student could use the equipment in **Figure 1** to investigate how changing the temperature affects the rate of anaerobic respiration in yeast. [4 marks]

> **HINT** A water bath can be used to change the temperature of the flask.

_____

_____

_____

_____

_____

_____

_____

_____

02.2 The student plotted his results as a line graph, as shown in **Figure 2**.

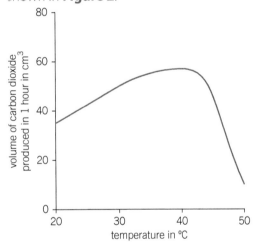

Figure 2

Describe what the graph shows about how temperature affects the rate of anaerobic respiration in yeast. [3 marks]

> **HINT** To get the full marks, make sure you describe three different trends in the graph. Include numbers and units, such as: 'between a temperature of ... and ..., the rate ...'

_____

_____

_____

_____

B9 Checklist

	Student Book	☺	☺	☹
I can write the equations that summarise aerobic respiration.	9.1			
I can explain why cellular respiration is important.	9.1			
I can describe how my body responds to the increased demands for energy during exercise.	9.2			
I can explain why less energy is transferred by anaerobic respiration than by aerobic respiration.	9.3			
I can describe how anaerobic respiration can take place in lots of different organisms, including plants, bacteria, and fungi.	9.3			
I can define metabolism.	9.4			

B10.1 Principles of homeostasis

A Which of these are internal conditions controlled by homeostasis?

Tick the correct boxes.

V blood glucose concentration ☐

W heart rate ☐

X body temperature ☐

Y water content of the body ☐

Z blood oxygen concentration ☐

B Devin is exercising on a hot day. He does not stop to drink any water or eat any food.

Circle the correct **bold** words in the statements below to show what happens to his internal conditions.

a His body temperature **decreases/increases**.

b His blood water level **decreases/increases**.

c His blood glucose level **decreases/increases**.

Explain your answer to part **b**.

_____

_____

_____

_____

C Draw a line to match each key feature of a control system to its function.

Key feature	Function
receptors	muscles or glands that bring about a response
coordination centre	cells that detect stimuli (changes in the environment)
effectors	receives and processes information

What you need to remember

Homeostasis is the control of the _____ conditions of a cell or organism.

It is important for maintaining suitable conditions for cell functions, including enzyme action.

In the human body homeostasis includes control of blood _____ concentration, body temperature, and water levels. The control systems are automatic and may involve _____ or chemical responses.

All control systems include _____ , coordination centres, and effectors.

B10.2 The structure and function of the human nervous system

A Sense organs contain receptor cells.

Label the sense organs on the diagram. Choose the type of receptors they contain from the following list. Some sense organs will have more than one type of receptor.

sense organ

receptors it contains

change in temperature   light   chemical   sound   change in position   pressure   pain

B Jules catches a ball that is thrown towards her.

Choose from the words below to fill the gaps to explain how she does this.

nerve   message   neurone   glands   brain   eyes   motor   relay   muscles   impulse

The light receptors in her _____ detect the movement of the ball. Information is sent as an electrical

_____ along a sensory _____ until it reaches the central nervous system (CNS). The CNS is

made up of the brain and the spinal cord.

The _____ coordinates the response and sends impulses out along _____ neurones to the

arm _____ , which contract to move the arms towards the ball.

C Effectors carry out a response to an impulse.

Which of these are effectors?

Tick the correct boxes.

W neurones   ☐   **Y** glands   ☐

X muscles   ☐   **Z** brain   ☐

What you need to remember

The nervous system uses _____ impulses to enable you to react quickly to your surroundings and
coordinate your behaviour. Cells called receptors detect _____ (changes in the environment).
Impulses from receptors pass along _____ neurones to the central nervous system (CNS), which is
made up of the brain and _____ cord. The brain coordinates the response, and impulses are sent
along _____ neurones from the brain to the effector organs.
Effector organs may be _____ or glands.

B10.3 Reflex actions

A Reflex actions are automatic and rapid.

Which of these are reflex actions?
Tick the correct boxes.

L talking ☐

M dropping a hot pan ☐

N picking up a phone when it rings ☐

O blinking ☐

B Statements **P–Q** describe how an electrical impulse travels from neurone **X** to neurone **Y** across a synapse (gap). However, they are in the wrong order.

P Chemicals are released into the gap.

Q Chemicals bind with receptors on the surface of neurone **Y**.

R An impulse arrives at the end of neurone **X**.

S A new electrical impulse is set up in neurone **Y**.

T Chemicals diffuse across the gap.

Write the letters in the correct order in the boxes below.

☐ ☐ ☐ ☐ ☐

C The diagram opposite shows the pathway of a reflex action (a reflex arc).

Write the letter (**U–Z**) that shows:

a sensory neurone ☐   a receptor ☐

a motor neurone ☐   an effector ☐

a relay neurone ☐   a synapse ☐

white matter
grey matter

What you need to remember

Reflex actions are _____ and rapid and do not involve the conscious parts of the _____ .

They control everyday bodily functions, such as breathing and digestion, and help you to avoid

_____ . The main stages of a reflex arc are:

stimulus → receptor → sensory neurone → _____ neurone → motor neurone →

_____ → response

At junctions between neurones are tiny gaps called _____ . Impulses travel across them using

_____ that diffuse across the gap.

B10 Practice questions

01 A person touches a hot saucepan. Their hand immediately moves away.

Which of these statements about this action are correct?

Tick **two** boxes. [2 marks]

HINT A voluntary action is something that you choose to do. The opposite of voluntary is automatic.

W It is voluntary. ☐

X It is automatic. ☐

Y It is a reflex action. ☐

Z It is brought about by hormones. ☐

02 **Figure 1** shows two neurones involved in the action described in **01**.

neurone **A**   neurone **B**

 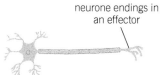

neurone endings in an effector

receptor

Figure 1

HINT There are three neurones involved: sensory, relay, and motor.

02.1 Name neurone **A**. [1 mark]

_____

02.2 Name neurone **B**. [1 mark]

_____

02.3 Draw an arrow next to each neurone in **Figure 1** to show the direction of impulses. [2 marks]

03 The impulses travel along these neurones at a speed of 120 m/s.

03.1 Calculate how long it would take an impulse to travel 3 m. [2 marks]

HINT $speed = \dfrac{distance}{time}$. You can rearrange this to give $time = \dfrac{distance}{speed}$.

_____ s

03.2 Explain why it is important that the impulses travel quickly. [2 marks]

_____

_____

_____

04 Neurones in the nervous system are separated by tiny gaps.

Figure 2 shows this.

neurone **C**

impulse arrives in neurone

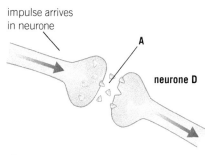

A

neurone **D**

Figure 2

04.1 Name the gap labelled **A** in **Figure 2**. [1 mark]

_____

04.2 Electrical impulses cannot cross the gap labelled **A**. Use **Figure 2** to explain how a new electrical impulse is started up in neurone **D**. [3 marks]

HINT Chemicals can travel across the gap by diffusion.

_____

_____

_____

_____

B10 Checklist

	Student Book	☺	☺	☹
I can explain why it is important to control the internal environment.	10.1			
I can name the key elements of control systems.	10.1			
I can explain why we need a nervous system.	10.2			
I can explain how the structure of the nervous system is adapted to its function.	10.2			
I can explain how receptors enable us to respond to changes in our surroundings.	10.2			
I can explain what reflexes are.	10.3			
I can describe how reflexes work.	10.3			
I can explain why reflexes are important in the body.	10.3			

B11.1 Principles of hormonal control

A The diagram opposite shows the main endocrine glands of the human body.

Draw lines to match each letter on the diagram to the gland and to the name of **one** hormone that it secretes.

Letter	Gland	Hormone it secretes
R	adrenal gland	oestrogen
S	ovary (female)	FSH (in women)
T	pancreas	thyroxine
U	thyroid gland	testosterone
V	testis (male)	adrenaline
W	pituitary gland	insulin

B Circle the correct **bold** words in the sentences below to compare typical nervous and hormonal responses.

Most hormonal responses are **slower/quicker** than nervous ones.

Hormonal effects are usually **longer/shorter** lasting than nervous ones.

C Which statement best explains why the pituitary gland is known as the master gland?

Tick the correct box.

X It secretes hormones that affect other glands. ☐

Y It secretes the strongest hormones. ☐

Z It is located in the brain. ☐

What you need to remember

The _____ system is made up of glands that secrete chemicals called _____ directly into the bloodstream. The blood carries the hormone to a _____ organ where it produces an effect.

Compared with the _____ system, the effects of hormones are often slower but longer lasting.

The pituitary gland is the _____ gland and secretes several hormones, some of which act on other glands.

B11.2 The control of blood glucose levels

A Draw a line to match each key word to its meaning.

Key word

| glucose |
| glycogen |
| insulin |
| pancreas |

Meaning

| a hormone that allows glucose to move from the blood into cells |
| the sugar used in respiration |
| a gland that secretes insulin |
| a storage carbohydrate found in the liver and muscles |

B Complete the flow diagram opposite to show what happens after you eat a meal.

Use the sentences below.

Glucose moves from the blood into the cells.

The pancreas secretes insulin into the bloodstream.

Blood glucose levels decrease.

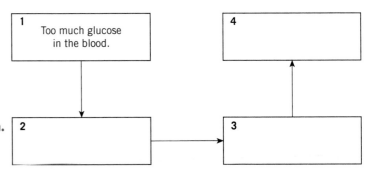

1 | Too much glucose in the blood.

4

2

3

C There are two types of diabetes.

Draw a line from each statement to show if it is describing type 1 or type 2 diabetes.

Statement

| type 1 diabetes |

| rare in children |
| the most common form of diabetes |
| the pancreas stops producing insulin |
| body cells don't respond properly to insulin |
| obesity is a risk factor |
| becoming more common in the UK |

| type 2 diabetes |

What you need to remember

Your blood glucose levels are monitored and controlled by your _____ . This organ produces the hormone _____ , which allows glucose to move from the blood into the cells and to be stored as _____ in the liver and muscles.

In type _____ diabetes, the blood glucose may rise to fatally high levels because the pancreas does not secrete enough insulin. In type _____ diabetes, the body stops responding to its own insulin.

B11.3 Treating diabetes

A Two people were given a drink high in glucose and their blood glucose levels were monitored.

The graph below shows the results.

a Which person, **X** or **Y**, has diabetes? _____

b Explain how you made your decision.

_____

_____

_____

_____

B Type 1 diabetes cannot be cured, but it can be treated.

Explain what this means.

_____

_____

_____

_____

C Tick the boxes to show if each treatment below is used to treat type 1 or type 2 diabetes.

Treatment	Type 1	Type 2
W control the amount of carbohydrate eaten	☐	☐
X insulin injections	☐	☐
Y dialysis	☐	☐
Z drugs to help the pancreas make more insulin	☐	☐

What you need to remember

Type 1 diabetes is normally controlled by injecting _____ to replace the hormone that is not made in the body.

Type 2 diabetes is often treated by controlling the amount of _____ in the diet and taking more _____ . If this doesn't work, _____ may be needed.

B11.5 Human reproduction

A Label the diagram of the female reproductive system opposite using these words:

ovary   cervix   uterus   fallopian tube   vagina

B Draw a line to match each part of the male reproductive system to its function.

Part	Function
testes	carries sperm to the penis
scrotum	keeps the testes away from the body for maximum sperm production
sperm duct	makes sperm
penis	places sperm into the vagina

C Which of these are hormones involved in the menstrual cycle?

Tick the correct boxes.

S testosterone ☐

T progesterone ☐

U oestrogen ☐

V insulin ☐

D During puberty both boys and girls develop secondary sexual characteristics.

Tick the boxes to show which characteristics occur in boys and which in girls.

Secondary sexual characteristic	Boys	Girls
W growth of underarm hair	☐	☐
X fat deposited on hips	☐	☐
Y brain changes and matures	☐	☐
Z shoulders and chest broaden	☐	☐

What you need to remember

During _____ reproductive hormones cause secondary _____ characteristics to develop. Oestrogen is the main female reproductive hormone produced by the _____ . At puberty eggs begin to mature and one is released approximately every 28 days during a process called _____ .
Hormones involved in the _____ cycle of a woman include _____ stimulating hormone (FSH), luteinising hormone (LH), oestrogen, and _____ .
_____ is the main male reproductive hormone produced by the _____ . It stimulates sperm production.

B11.7 The artificial control of fertility

A There are different types of contraceptive. For each one listed below:

- write **H** in the box if it is hormone-based
- write **B** if it uses the barrier method
- write **O** if it uses another method.

The first one has been done for you.

contraceptive pill	**H**
condoms	
vasectomy	
contraceptive implant	
diaphragm	

B Study the chart opposite.

For each of the following conclusions based on the chart, circle **true** or **false**.

a The most effective form of contraceptive on the chart is spermicides. **true/false**

b With no contraception around 85% of women had an unexpected pregnancy. **true/false**

c If a couple use a condom there is a chance that the woman could become pregnant. **true/false**

d Hormonal contraceptives are more effective than non-hormonal ones. **true/false**

proportion of women with unexpected pregnancy in first year of use

C A couple is deciding which contraceptive to use. Why can't science alone answer this question?

Tick the correct box.

W There is no data on which contraceptive is the most effective. ☐

X Scientists do not understand how contraceptives work. ☐

Y There are too many different choices. ☐

Z Personal views and beliefs have to be taken into account. ☐

What you need to remember

To prevent pregnancy you need to prevent the egg and _____ meeting, or prevent a fertilised egg implanting in the _____ . This is known as contraception.

Hormone-based contraceptives include oral contraceptives (the _____), implants, injections, and patches. Spermicides kill _____ – this is a chemical method.

_____ methods prevent the sperm reaching the egg. Methods include _____ and diaphragms. Other methods of contraception are intrauterine devices, _____ (not having sexual intercourse), and surgical sterilisation.

B11 Practice questions

01.1 Choose the correct words from the list below to complete the sentences about hormonal control. [2 marks]

blood   **effect**   **endocrine**   **glands**
impulses   **nervous**   **organ**

The _____ system is made up of _____ that secrete chemicals called hormones.

Each hormone is carried by the _____ to its target organ where it produces an

_____.

01.2 Draw a line to match each hormone to its function. [2 marks]

Hormone	Function
oestrogen	involved in the control of blood glucose levels
insulin	causes eggs in the ovary to mature
testosterone	main male reproductive hormone
FSH	main female reproductive hormone

01.3 Determine where the hormone oestrogen is made. [1 mark]

HINT Which gland produces hormones in the female reproductive system?

_____

02 **Figure 1** shows the changing levels of the female sex hormones during the menstrual cycle.

0   5   12   16   20   28 **days**
old egg leaves body in   egg released   new egg in womb
menstrual flow

0   12   15   23   **days**
new egg maturing in ovary   new egg travelling to womb

Figure 1

Describe the main stages of the menstrual cycle and when they occur. Explain how FSH, LH, and oestrogen control the changes. [6 marks]

HINT When answering six-mark questions, add as much detail as you can to your answer. Write in full sentences and use correct scientific terminology.

B11 Checklist

	Student Book	☺	😐	☹
I can define the word hormone.	11.1			
I can name the main organs of the endocrine system.	11.1			
I can describe the role of the pituitary gland.	11.1			83
I can describe the role of the pancreas in monitoring and controlling blood glucose concentration.	11.2			
I can explain how insulin controls blood glucose levels in the body.	11.2			
I can explain what causes diabetes.	11.2			
I can describe the differences in the ways type 1 and type 2 diabetes are treated.	11.3			
I can name the main human reproductive hormones.	11.4			
I can describe how hormones control the changes at puberty.	11.4			
I can name methods of hormonal and non-hormonal contraception.	11.7			

B12.1 Types of reproduction

A Tick the columns to show which statements are true for **asexual reproduction** and which are true for **sexual reproduction**. Some are true for both types of reproduction.

Statements	✓ if true for asexual reproduction	✓ if true for sexual reproduction
Genetic material is passed from parent to offspring.		
Involves two parents.		
The offspring are clones of the parent.		
The offspring are genetically different from each other.		
The offspring are formed by fertilisation.		
Requires sperm and egg cells in animals.		
Requires pollen and egg cells in flowering plants.		

B Circle **asexual** or **sexual** for each type of reproduction described below.

a yeast budding **asexual/sexual**

b formation of a human zygote **asexual/sexual**

c human skin cells multiplying **asexual/sexual**

d poppy seeds forming from the joining of pollen and ovule **asexual/sexual**

C Which of these statements is an advantage of sexual reproduction over asexual reproduction?

Tick the correct box.

W The offspring show more variation. ☐

X It is quicker. ☐

Y It requires two parents. ☐

Z Gametes are formed. ☐

What you need to remember

Asexual reproduction involves _____ parent. There is no joining (fusion) of _____ cells (gametes). The offspring are formed by mitosis so they are all genetically _____ to their parent and each other. They are clones.

Gametes are formed during a type of cell division called _____ . In _____ reproduction male and female gametes fuse. There is a mixing of genetic information that leads to _____ in the offspring.

B12.2 Cell division in sexual reproduction

A Draw a line to match each key word to its meaning.

Key word	Meaning
mitosis	a sex cell (sperm and egg in humans)
meiosis	the joining of a male and female sex cell
gamete	cell division that produces identical cells
fertilisation	a section of DNA
gene	cell division that produces gametes

B The diagram below shows the process of meiosis.

Write the correct letter in each cell to show how many chromosomes are present. The first one has been done for you.

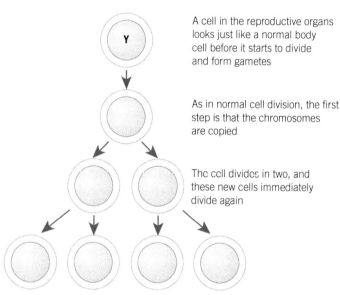

A cell in the reproductive organs looks just like a normal body cell before it starts to divide and form gametes

As in normal cell division, the first step is that the chromosomes are copied

The cell divides in two, and these new cells immediately divide again

This gives four sex cells, each with a single set of chromosomes – in this case two instead of the original four

C Write the correct number of chromosomes in each of the following human cells.

skin cell _____

sperm cell _____

zygote _____

egg cell _____

ovary cell _____

What you need to remember

Cells in the reproductive organs divide by _____ to form the gametes (sex cells).

Body cells have _____ sets of chromosomes, gametes have only one set.

In meiosis, the genetic material is copied and then the cell _____ twice to form _____ genetically different gametes, each with a single set of chromosomes.

Gametes join at _____ to form a cell with the normal number of chromosomes. The new cell divides by _____ . The number of cells increases and as the embryo develops, the cells differentiate.

B12.3 DNA and the genome

A Circle each correct word to describe the relationship between DNA, genes, and chromosomes.

Your genetic information is stored on a long molecule called

DNA
genes
chromosomes

which is packaged into

DNA
genes
chromosomes

, small sections of which are called

DNA
genes
chromosomes

B Match each label on the diagram to the correct word below.

Write **S**, **T**, **U**, or **V** beside each word.

gene ☐

chromosome ☐

cell ☐

nucleus ☐

C What is a genome?

Tick the correct box.

W the number of chromosomes in each cell ☐

X the entire genetic material of the organism ☐

Y the genetic material in the mitochondria ☐

Z the function of each gene in the organism's DNA ☐

D Name **one** benefit of studying the human genome.

_____

_____

_____

What you need to remember

The genetic material in the nucleus of a cell is composed of DNA. DNA is a _____ made up of two strands forming a _____ helix.

A gene is a small section of DNA on a _____ . Each gene codes for a particular sequence of amino acids, to make a specific _____ .

The _____ of an organism is the entire genetic material of that organism. The whole human genome has now been studied and this will have great importance for medicine in the future.

B12.4 Inheritance in action

A Solve the clues to work out the key words.

Then find them in the wordsearch below.

```
E  G  B  W  R  L  L  N  G  Y  V  H
P  P  D  J  S  F  I  C  K  E  E  D
Y  L  Y  U  F  E  C  T  A  T  N  R
T  V  N  T  T  Q  Z  K  E  N  Y  E
O  N  O  O  O  V  X  R  N  O  L  T
N  C  R  Q  Y  N  O  B  S  I  N  T
E  P  R  M  A  Z  E  N  Z  Z  M  L
G  K  I  X  Y  Z  T  H  U  C  X  P
P  Y  X  G  Z  L  W  E  P  M  H  K
F  P  O  M  J  A  J  U  W  O  C  C
W  U  F  M  C  U  A  L  L  E  L  E
S  X  S  U  O  G  Y  Z  O  M  O  H
```

A section of DNA that codes for one protein. _____

Different forms of a gene. _____

An individual with two identical alleles for a characteristic. _____

An individual with different alleles for a characteristic. _____

Made up of many amino acids joined together. _____

Describes the alleles that an individual has. _____

Describes the physical appearance of an individual. _____

B The coat of a dog may be straight (H) or curly (h).

Draw a line to match each description to the correct genotype.

Description		Genotype
a heterozygous genotype		HH
a genotype for the phenotype curly hair		Hh
a homozygous dominant genotype		hh

What you need to remember

Some characteristics are controlled by a single gene. Each gene may have different forms called

_____ .

The _____ is the alleles present (e.g., BB). The _____ describes a trait (e.g., black fur).

If the two alleles are the _____ , the individual is homozygous for that trait. If the alleles are different,

the individual is _____ . A _____ allele, shown as a capital letter, is always expressed

in the phenotype, even if only one copy is present. A _____ allele, shown as a lower case letter, is

only expressed if _____ copies are present. Most characteristics are the result of multiple genes

interacting, rather than a single gene.

B12.5 More about genetics

A Fruit flies can have red eyes (E) or orange eyes (e).

The genetic diagram opposite shows the possible offspring between two fruit flies.

Use the genetic diagram to circle whether each statement below is **true** or **false**.

Gametes	E	e
e	Ee	ee
e	Ee	ee

a Both parents have red eyes.   **true/false**

b It is possible for an orange-eyed fly to have offspring with red eyes.   **true/false**

c The proportion of offspring that has the genotype Ee is 25%.   **true/false**

d The proportion of offspring that has the phenotype red eyes is 50%.   **true/false**

e The ratio of red-eyed offspring to orange-eyed offspring is 1:1.   **true/false**

B Human sex chromosomes are X and Y.

Write the correct pair of sex chromosome in the circle on each person.

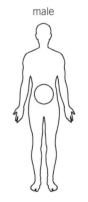
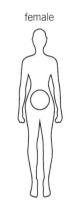

male   female

C Earlobes can be attached to the head or free.
The diagram opposite shows a family tree.

Having attached earlobes may be caused by a recessive allele. How does the family tree provide evidence for this?

HINT Look at the children of people 6 and 7.

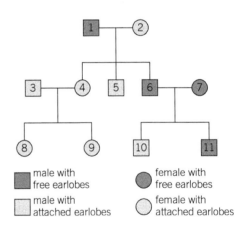

male with free earlobes
female with free earlobes
male with attached earlobes
female with attached earlobes

_____

_____

_____

_____

_____

What you need to remember

_____ squares and family trees are used to show genetic crosses. They show the possible genotypes and _____ of offspring. Direct proportion and _____ can be used to express the outcome of a genetic cross.

Ordinary human body cells contain _____ pairs of chromosomes. 22 control general body characteristics. The _____ chromosomes carry the genes that determine sex. Human females have two _____ chromosomes. In _____ the sex chromosomes are different (XY).

B12.6 Inherited disorders

A Some disorders are inherited.

Write a letter and a number next to each inherited disorder to show how it affects the body (**U–W**) and how it is inherited (**1** or **2**).

How it affects the body

U	areas in the body get clogged up by thick mucus

V	extra fingers or toes

W	affects the nervous system

How it is inherited

1	a dominant allele from either parent

2	two recessive alleles from both parents

Inherited disorders:

polydactyly _____   cystic fibrosis _____   Huntington's disease _____

B Aris has polydactyly. What could his genotype be?

Tick all the correct boxes.

X PP ☐

Y Pp ☐

Z pp ☐

C Maddy has cystic fibrosis. Her body produces thick mucus in some organs.

Draw a line to match each part of her body to the effect of the disease on her health.

Part of the body
lungs

small intestine

fallopian tubes

Effect
difficulty digesting food

reduction in oxygen reaching her bloodstream

fertility problems

What you need to remember

Some disorders are caused by a change in the DNA. They can be passed from parent to child. These are _____ disorders.

If a person has _____ they are born with extra fingers or toes. It is a dominant phenotype caused by a _____ allele that can be inherited from either or both parents.

Cystic fibrosis causes thick _____ to build up in the lungs and the digestive and reproductive systems. It is a recessive phenotype and is caused by _____ alleles that must be inherited from _____ parents.

B12.7 Screening for genetic disorders

A To carry out screening, cells from the unborn baby need to be tested. The diagrams opposite show the two main methods used.

Tick the columns to show which statements are true for each method.

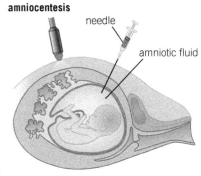

chorionic villus sampling –
transabdominal method

needle

placenta

amniocentesis

needle

amniotic fluid

	✓ if true for chorionic villus sampling	✓ if true for amniocentesis
carried out between 10 and 12 weeks		
carried out between 15 and 16 weeks		
needle inserted into the baby		
needle inserted through the wall of the uterus		
cells taken from the placenta		
cells taken from the amniotic fluid		
associated with a small risk of miscarriage		

B Couples may choose to use IVF and screen the embryos.

Write the letters in the boxes below to show the correct order of steps in this method.

V Leave the embryos to grow until they are balls of cells.

W Place the embryos that do not have the genetic disorder into the mother's uterus where they can develop.

X Remove eggs from the mother's ovaries.

Y Mix the eggs with sperm from the father in a dish.

Z Take one cell from each embryo and test for genetic disorders.

☐ ☐ ☐ ☐ ☐

What you need to remember

Cells from embryos and _____ can be screened during pregnancy for the _____ that cause many genetic disorders. The main methods for taking the cells include amniocentesis and chorionic _____ sampling. Both have a risk of _____.

Some couples may decide to use _____ to create embryos outside the body. These are then tested before being implanted into the mother, so only babies without the disorder are born.

Screening raises economic, social, and _____ issues.

B12 Practice questions

01 In human reproduction gametes join together.

01.1 Name this type of reproduction. [1 mark]

_____

01.2 The flow diagram in **Figure 1** represents human reproduction.

```
┌──────────────┐        ┌──────────────┐
│ cell in ovary│        │ cell in testis│
└──────────────┘        └──────────────┘
        │                       │
    ┌───────────────────────────────┐
    │               A               │
    └───────────────────────────────┘
        │                       │
┌──────────────┐        ┌──────────────┐
│   egg cell   │        │  sperm cell  │
└──────────────┘        └──────────────┘
        │                       │
    ┌───────────────────────────────┐
    │               B               │
    └───────────────────────────────┘
                    │
            ┌──────────────┐
            │    cell X    │
            └──────────────┘
```

Figure 1

A and **B** are processes involved in human reproduction.

Draw a line from each letter to the name of the process it represents. [2 marks]

	fertilisation
A	meiosis
B	mitosis
	replication

01.3 Name cell **X** in **Figure 1**. [1 mark]

_____

01.4 In each box, write the number of chromosomes found in the nucleus of the cell. [3 marks]

HINT Human body cells have 23 **pairs** of chromosomes. Human sex cells (gametes) have 23 **single** chromosomes.

X cell in ovary ☐

Y egg cell ☐

Z cell **X** ☐

02 The sex chromosomes determine the sex of a person.

Complete the Punnett square in **Figure 2** to show sex inheritance.

Use it to explain why the ratio of men and women in the world is approximately 1:1. [3 marks]

HINT In human females the sex chromosomes are the same (XX). In human males the sex chromosomes are different (XY).

		Sperm	
Gametes	X		
Egg	X		
	X	XX	XY

Figure 2

_____

_____

_____

B12 Checklist

	Student Book	☺	☺	☹
I can identify the main differences between asexual and sexual reproduction.	12.1			
I can describe how cells divide by meiosis to form gametes.	12.2			
I can describe how meiosis halves the number of chromosomes in gametes and fertilisation restores the full number.	12.2			
I can explain how sexual reproduction gives rise to variation.	12.2			
I can describe how DNA is the material of inheritance.	12.3			
I can define the term genome.	12.3			
I can outline some of the benefits of studying the human genome.	12.3			
I can identify different forms of genes, called alleles, as either dominant or recessive.	12.4			
I can predict the results of genetic crosses when a characteristic is controlled by a single gene.	12.4			
I can interpret Punnett square diagrams.	12.4			
I can use proportion and ratios to express the outcome of a genetic cross.	12.5			
I can describe how sex is inherited.	12.5			
I can interpret a family tree.	12.5			
I can describe how the human genetic disorders polydactyly and cystic fibrosis are inherited.	12.6			
I can recall that embryos are screened for some of the alleles that cause genetic disorders.	12.7			
I can describe some of the concerns and issues associated with these screening processes.	12.7			

B13.1 Variation

A Variation between individuals may be due to genetics, the environment, or both.

Draw a line to match each human variation to its cause.

Variation		Cause
eye colour ●		genetics
height ●		
accent ●		environment
pierced ears ●		
blood group ●		a combination of both
skin colour ●		

B Which of these are environmental conditions that will affect variation in plants?

Tick the correct boxes.

W amount of light ☐

X concentration of minerals in the soil ☐

Y concentration of oxygen in the air ☐

Z temperature ☐

C A scientist carried out a study. His hypothesis was: 'Type 1 diabetes is caused only by genetics.'

He studied identical twins. In 85% of the pairs of twins studied, if one twin had type 1 diabetes then the other twin also had diabetes.

a Does this evidence support his hypothesis? _____

b Explain your answer.

_____

_____

_____

What you need to remember

_____ is the differences in the characteristics of individuals in a population. It may be due to differences in the _____ inherited from parents (genetic causes), the conditions in which organisms develop (_____ causes), or a combination of _____ .

Studying identical _____ helps scientists to understand what controls different characteristics.

If a characteristic is very similar in identical twins, then it is more likely to be caused by _____ . If a characteristic is very different, it is more likely to be influenced by the _____ .

B13.2 Evolution by natural selection

A What is a mutation?

Tick the correct box.

S an organism that has special characteristics ☐

T a chemical or radiation that damages cells ☐

U a change in the DNA code ☐

V differences between individuals ☐

B In a population of mice some individuals have better eyesight than others.

Explain how this gives them a better chance of survival.

_____

_____

_____

C One example of natural selection is the increase in bacteria that are resistant to antibiotics. This means that they cannot be killed by antibiotics.

The stages in how this happens are shown below. They are in the wrong order.

W Antibiotics are used on the population. The resistant bacteria are not killed.

X A few bacteria in a population have a new allele that makes them resistant to antibiotics.

Y The population of resistant bacteria increases. There are now more resistant bacteria than non-resistant ones.

Z The resistant bacteria reproduce to form genetically identical offspring.

Write a letter next to each stage of natural selection to match it to the correct statement.

Stage of natural selection

mutation of a gene ☐   advantage to survival ☐

breed ☐   pass on genes ☐

What you need to remember

The theory of evolution by _____ selection states that all species of living things have evolved from simple life forms that first developed over 3 _____ years ago.

Changes in the DNA are called _____ . They occur continuously. Very rarely this leads to a new phenotype. This may form individuals that are more suited to an _____ change. They are likely to survive and _____ successfully. These alleles are then passed on to the next generation. This can lead to a relatively rapid change in the species.

If two populations of a species become so different that they can no longer interbreed to form _____ offspring, they have formed two new _____ .

B13.3 Selective breeding

A Wheat is an important food crop that is grown on farms.

Describe **two** useful characteristics of wheat.

1 _____

   _____

2 _____

   _____

B Humans have been carrying out selective breeding for thousands of years since they first bred food crops from wild plants and domesticated animals.

The flow diagram below shows how a farmer uses selective breeding.

Fill in the blank box to describe this stage.

The farmer has many animals which show variation.	→	

The animals are bred to produce offspring.

C Draw lines to match the organism to the features that have been selectively bred for.

Organism

tomato plant

dog

rose

pig

Feature

brightly coloured flowers

resistance to disease

obedience

more muscle

D Describe **one** problem caused by the selective breeding of dogs.

_____

_____

B13.4 Genetic engineering

A What is a genetically modified (GM) crop? Tick the correct box.

W a crop that is resistant to diseases ☐

X a crop that has a new gene inserted into its genetic material ☐

Y a crop that has a mutation in its genetic material ☐

Z a crop that contains human genes ☐

B Many different organisms have been genetically modified.

For each genetic modification in the table below, tick the boxes to show which organism it has been used in. Some genetic modifications may have been used in more than one organism.

Genetic modification	✓ if used in bacteria	✓ if used in cows	✓ if used in crops
make human proteins			
more nutritional			
resistance to pests			
increase in yield			

C In the USA 158 million hectares of land is taken up growing maize. 55 million acres of this is GM maize.

Calculate the percentage of land used to grow GM maize.

What you need to remember

Genetic _____ involves modifying (changing) the genetic material of an organism. The _____ for a desirable characteristic is cut out of one organism and transferred to the genetic material of another organism. This gives the genetically engineered organism a new, desirable characteristic.

Plant crops have been genetically engineered to be _____ to certain diseases, or to produce bigger fruits. These are called genetically _____ (GM) crops.

B13.5 Ethics of genetic technologies

A Which of these are uses of genetic engineering?

Underline the ones that are uses.

N production of crops resistant to pests

O making many copies of plants to sell

P increasing the nutritional value of food

Q preserving rare plant species

B Scientists are exploring ways of putting 'healthy' genes into affected cells so the cells work properly.

a Tick the correct box to name this type of genetic modification.

R selective breeding ☐

S natural selection ☐

T gene therapy ☐

U IVF ☐

b Name **one** disorder that could be cured in this way.

_____   _____

C Genetic modification has many benefits and possible risks. Some are listed below.

Write a **B** in each box next to a statement that is describing a benefit.

Write an **R** in each box next to a statement that is describing a possible risk.

W transferring modified genes to other organisms ☐

X increasing crop yields ☐

Y growing rice that contains vitamin A ☐

Z harm to human health ☐

What you need to remember

Scientists are exploring the use of genetic modification to put 'healthy' genes into affected cells and overcome some _____ disorders.

There are _____ and risks associated with genetic engineering in agriculture and medicine.

One benefit is that growing GM crops can _____ food production.

One _____ is that genes from GM crops might spread to wildlife.

Some people are worried about genetic engineering being used to create _____ babies with particular characteristics such as high intelligence. These are ethical objections.

B13 Practice questions

01 A student carried out a survey in her local town centre.

She asked people if they were concerned about growing GM (genetically modified) crops in the UK.

01.1 Describe the difference between a normal crop and a GM crop. [1 mark]

_____

_____

01.2 She started to plot her results as a bar chart, shown in **Figure 1**.

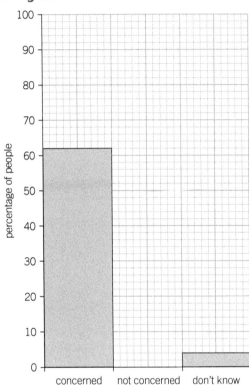

Figure 1

Calculate the percentage of people who were not concerned about GM crops. [2 marks]

_____%

01.3 Show your answer to **01.2** on the bar chart. [1 mark]

01.4 Give **two** reasons why some people are concerned about growing GM crops. [2 marks]

HINT Consider both environmental and ethical concerns.

1 _____

_____

2 _____

_____

02 A student placed five cloned seedlings (they had the same genes) in areas with different light levels.

After 8 weeks he measured the height of each plant and recorded the colour of the flowers.

Table 1 shows his results.

Table 1

Plant	Height in cm	Colour of flowers
A	34.3	white
B	19.4	white
C	36.2	white
D	12.6	white
E	25.8	white

02.1 Name **one** control variable that he should use in his investigation. [1 mark]

_____

02.2 Identify the range in height of the plants. [1 mark]

HINT The range is the maximum and minimum values. For example, a range of lengths would be written as 'from 10 cm to 50 cm'.

_____

_____

_____

02.3 Circle the type of variation showed by each characteristic. Explain your answers. [4 marks]

Characteristic: Height

Variation: **environmental/genetic**

Explanation:

_____

_____

_____

Characteristic: Colour of flower

Variation: **environmental/genetic**

Explanation:

_____

_____

B13 Checklist

	Student Book	☺	☺	☹
I can explain what makes someone different from the rest of their family.	13.1			
I can explain why identical twins are not exactly the same in every way.	13.1			
I can describe how natural selection works.	13.2			
I can explain how evolution occurs via natural selection.	13.2			
I can define selective breeding.	13.3			
I can describe how selective breeding works.	13.3			
I can evaluate selective breeding by considering the benefits and risks.	13.3			
I can evaluate the potential benefits and problems associated with genetic engineering in agriculture and medicine.	13.4			
I can evaluate some of the concerns and uncertainties about the new genetic technologies, such as cloning and genetic engineering.	13.5			

B14.1 Evidence for evolution

A Fossils are good evidence for the theory of evolution by natural selection.

a Name the scientist who proposed this theory.

_____

b What extra evidence is also now available to support this theory?

Tick **one** box.

W Not all organisms form fossils. ☐   **Y** Many scientists agree that the theory is correct. ☐

X Characteristics are passed from parents to ☐   **Z** Species become extinct. ☐
offspring in genes.

B Number the sentences in the correct order to show one way in which fossils are formed.

The first one has been done for you.

	The flesh rots, leaving the skeleton.
	Over millions of years minerals replace the bone tissue.
1	An animal dies and falls to the ground.
	Layers of sediment build up over the skeleton.

C The timescales we use when talking about evolution are very large, so we show them using standard form.

Draw a line to match each timescale to the same number in standard form.

Timescale		Standard form
1 000 000 years		10^5 years
100 million years		10^6 years
100 thousand years		10^8 years
1 billion years		10^9 years

What you need to remember

Fossils are the remains of organisms from _____ of years ago that can be found in _____,
ice, and other places. They may be formed in different ways including being preserved so they do not
_____ , parts being replaced by _____ as they decay, and as preserved traces of
organisms such as footprints.

Fossils help us build up a picture of life on Earth long ago. But scientists cannot be certain how
_____ on Earth started. The fossil record is not complete for several reasons:

- Early forms of life were _____ -bodied so left few traces behind.

- The right conditions for fossil formation were rare.

- Many fossils have been destroyed by _____ activity, such as volcanoes.

- Not all fossils have been found.

B14.2 Fossils and extinction

A Modern-day crocodiles are very similar to their ancestors that lived millions of years ago.

Tick the box next to the statement that explains why.

X They did not want to evolve. ☐

Y Their environment has not changed very much. ☐

Z They have no predators. ☐

B Living organisms can change an environment and cause extinction in many ways.

Draw a line to match each cause of extinction to the correct example.

Cause of extinction

| new disease |

| successful competition |

| new predator |

Example

| hedgehogs on North Uist eating seabird eggs |

| Australian Tasmanian devil dying from a form of communicable cancer |

| rabbits in Australia breeding quickly |

C The bar graph opposite shows the number of animal extinctions that took place from the 17th century to the 20th century.

a Describe the trend in the graph.

_____

_____

b Suggest **one** reason for this.

_____

_____

What you need to remember

You can learn from _____ how much or how little organisms have changed as life has developed on Earth.

_____ is the permanent loss of all members of a _____. It may be caused by a number of factors including a change in temperature, new _____ that can wipe out prey animals, new diseases, or new, more successful competitors.

B14.3 More about extinction

A Circle the changes that could cause a mass extinction event.

new predator   **volcanic eruption**   **increase in temperature at the poles**   **meteor hitting the Earth**

B Some scientists think that 65 million years ago a giant asteroid collided with the Earth.

Tick the box next to the correct explanation of why this could have caused the dinosaurs to become extinct.

W The asteroid crushed them all.   ☐

X The dust thrown up darkened the sky so plants died.   ☐

Y The temperature of the Earth increased.   ☐

Z It caused floods to spread over the Earth.   ☐

C Other scientists have proposed a different theory for how the dinosaurs became extinct. They suggest that global temperatures decreased and the extinction happened very slowly.

a For each piece of evidence, draw a line to show which theory it supports.

Evidence

asteroid collision		decrease in temperature
	unexpected changes to fossils in Norway	
	huge crater in Chicxulub, Mexico	
	layers of crater debris in rocks that are 65 million years old	
	fossil record shows tropical vegetation was replaced by woodland plants	
	lots of iridium under the crater in Mexico	

b Explain why the asteroid collision is the most widely accepted theory.

_____

_____

_____

_____

_____

What you need to remember

Extinction can be caused by a variety of factors including changes to the environment over geological time and single catastrophic events, such as massive _____ eruptions or collisions with _____ .

During a _____ extinction, many of the species on Earth die out. The last mass extinction was when the _____ became extinct around 65 million years ago. Scientists have presented different theories for why this happened, with _____ to support them.

A Circle the correct **bold** words to explain what antibiotic resistant bacteria are.

Drugs called **antibiotics/antibodies** are used to kill bacteria. However they are becoming **less/more** useful over time. This is because strains of bacteria are evolving that are resistant to antibiotics. This means that the antibiotic **can/cannot** kill them.

This happens because some bacteria in a population have **carcinogens/mutations** that make them resistant. These bacteria **die/survive** and reproduce, so the population of resistant bacteria **decreases/increases**.

B Study the bar chart opposite. It shows the number of deaths in England and Wales in which MRSA played a part.

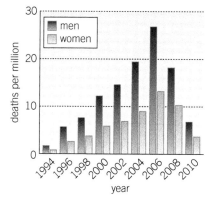

Tick the boxes next to the correct conclusions.

S More men than women died of MRSA infections. ☐

T The number of deaths from MRSA increased between 1994 and 2006. ☐

U The number of deaths from MRSA decreased between 2006 and 2010. ☐

V The lowest number of deaths from MRSA was in 2010. ☐

C There are several ways to stop the development of more strains of antibiotic resistant bacteria.

For each person below, suggest one thing they can do to help:

a person visiting a sick relative in a hospital

_____

b nurse working in a hospital

_____

c GP who prescribes drugs

_____

d person who has been given antibiotics

_____

What you need to remember

Bacteria can evolve quickly because they _____ at a fast rate.

Mutations can produce strains of bacteria that are resistant to _____ and so are not killed.
An example is _____ . Resistant strains survive and reproduce, so the population _____
by natural selection. The strain will then spread because people are not immune to it and there is no
effective treatment.

To reduce the rate of development of antibiotic resistant strains, it is important that _____ only
prescribe antibiotics when they need to, and patients use the antibiotics as prescribed and complete each
course. The use of antibiotics on farms should also be restricted. Scientists are developing new antibiotics but
this is _____ and slow.

B14.5 Classification

A Living things are classified into groups.

Number these classification groups in order of size.

The first one has been done for you.

[ ] species

[1] kingdom

[ ] genus

[ ] class

B Tick the boxes next to features that all plants share.

W They can move their whole body from place to place. [ ]

X Their cells have cell walls made of cellulose. [ ]

Y They can carry out photosynthesis. [ ]

Z All their cells contain chloroplasts. [ ]

C The polar bear has the scientific name *Ursus maritimus*.

Draw lines to match the names of the classification groups that the polar bear belongs to.

species		animal
kingdom		*maritimus*
genus		*Ursus*

What you need to remember

Carl _____ classified organisms into groups based on their features. The groups are kingdom, _____ , class, order, family, genus, and species. Organisms are named using the _____ system of genus and species.

As _____ improved, scientists had new evidence of the internal structures of organisms. Our understanding of genomes also improved. These developments led scientists to propose new models of _____ .

B14.6 New systems of classification

A Work from scientists such as Carl Woese has resulted in the introduction of a new system of classification.

Write these words in the correct boxes on the diagram to show how living things are now classified.

plants   archaebacteria   bacteria

domain   protista   eukaryota

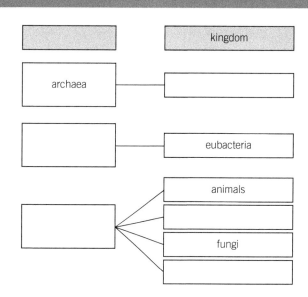

B A scientist uses a microscope to study a unicellular organism.

A labelled image of what they see is shown opposite.

a Name the domain that the organism belongs to.

_____

b Explain the reason for your answer.

_____

_____

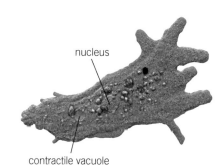

C The diagram opposite shows an evolutionary tree.

Use the information in the diagram to circle **true** or **false** for each statement.

a The closest relative of the lizard is the chimp.   **true/false**

b Lizards and humans do not share a common ancestor.   **true/false**

c There will be similarities in the DNA of all three organisms.
true/false

d The common ancestor of humans and chimps lived 5 million years ago.   **true/false**

e Humans evolved from chimps.   **true/false**

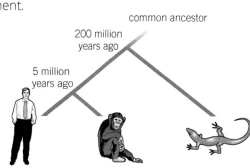

What you need to remember

A domain is a new, higher level of classification above _____.

Studying the similarities and differences between organisms allows us to classify them into the domains archaea, _____ , and eukaryota.

Classification helps us to understand evolutionary and ecological relationships.

Models such as evolutionary _____ allow us to suggest relationships between organisms.

B14 Practice questions

01 **Figure 1** shows the evolutionary tree of life.

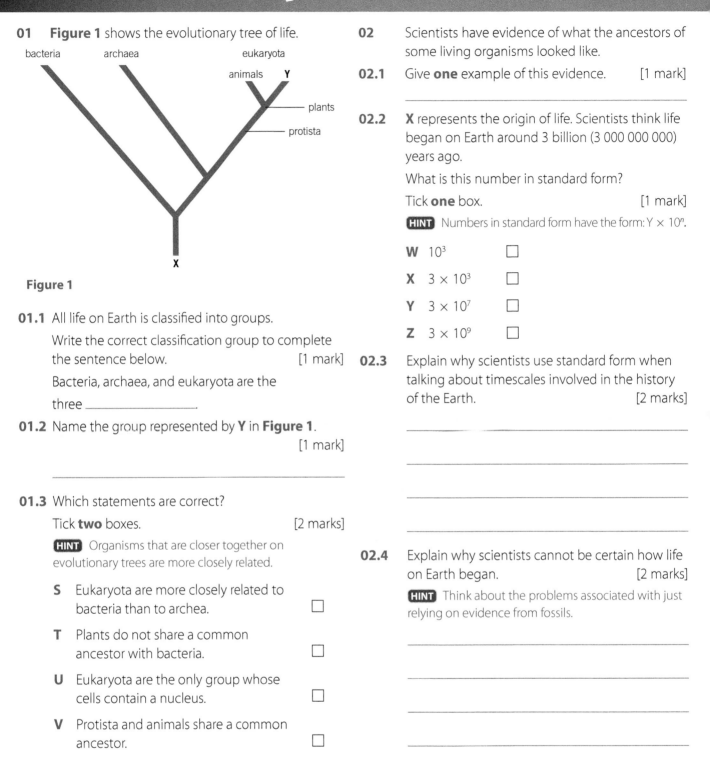

Figure 1

01.1 All life on Earth is classified into groups.

Write the correct classification group to complete the sentence below. [1 mark]

Bacteria, archaea, and eukaryota are the

three _____.

01.2 Name the group represented by **Y** in **Figure 1**. [1 mark]

_____

01.3 Which statements are correct?

Tick **two** boxes. [2 marks]

HINT Organisms that are closer together on evolutionary trees are more closely related.

S Eukaryota are more closely related to bacteria than to archea. ☐

T Plants do not share a common ancestor with bacteria. ☐

U Eukaryota are the only group whose cells contain a nucleus. ☐

V Protista and animals share a common ancestor. ☐

02 Scientists have evidence of what the ancestors of some living organisms looked like.

02.1 Give **one** example of this evidence. [1 mark]

_____

02.2 **X** represents the origin of life. Scientists think life began on Earth around 3 billion (3 000 000 000) years ago.

What is this number in standard form?

Tick **one** box. [1 mark]

HINT Numbers in standard form have the form: $Y \times 10^n$.

W 10^3 ☐

X 3×10^3 ☐

Y 3×10^7 ☐

Z 3×10^9 ☐

02.3 Explain why scientists use standard form when talking about timescales involved in the history of the Earth. [2 marks]

_____

_____

_____

_____

02.4 Explain why scientists cannot be certain how life on Earth began. [2 marks]

HINT Think about the problems associated with just relying on evidence from fossils.

_____

_____

_____

B14 Checklist

	Student Book	☺	😐	☹
I can give some evidence for the origins of life on Earth.	14.1			
I can describe how fossils are formed.	14.1			
I can describe what we can learn from fossils.	14.1			
I can explain what fossils can reveal about how organisms have changed over time.	14.2			
I can describe the ways that organisms can become extinct.	14.2			
I can describe how environmental change can cause extinction.	14.3			
I can describe how single catastrophic events can cause extinction on a massive scale.	12.3			
I can define antibiotic resistance.	14.4			
I can describe the part played by mutation in the development of antibiotic resistant strains of bacteria.	14.4			
I can describe how people can reduce the rate of development of antibiotic resistant strains such as MRSA.	14.4			
I can outline the basic principles of classification and the system developed by Linnaeus.	14.5			
I can use the binomial naming system of genus and species.	14.5			
I can describe how new technologies have changed classification.	14.5 14.6			
I can explain how scientists use evolutionary trees.	14.6			

B15.1 The importance of communities

A Draw a line to match the start of each definition to its end.

An ecosystem is made up of...	...populations of different species.
A community is...	...a non-living factor.
Interdependence is how...	...organisms interacting with non-living elements of their environment.
An abiotic factor is...	...different organisms rely on each other for food, shelter, etc.

B What is a stable community?

Tick the correct box.

W A community in which the numbers of organisms never change. ☐

X A community that contains only a few different organisms. ☐

Y A community in which the abiotic and biotic factors stay relatively constant. ☐

Z A community that can be easily replaced if it is lost. ☐

C Plants and animals need each other for survival.

Tick the correct boxes to show how.

You may need to tick more than one box for each row.

	Reproduction	Source of food	Source of materials for shelter
an example of how plants are dependent on animals			
an example of how animals are dependent on plants			

What you need to remember

The interaction of a community of living organisms with non-living (abiotic) parts is called an _____.
Organisms require materials from their surroundings to survive. They need other living organisms to help them reproduce, for _____, and for shelter. Plants require other organisms for pollination and _____ dispersal.

If one species is removed it can affect the whole community. This is called _____. A _____ community is one in which all the living organisms and abiotic parts are in balance so that population sizes remain fairly constant.

B15.2 Organisms in their environment

A Draw a line from each factor to show if it is an abiotic or a biotic factor.

Factor

light intensity
temperature
a new pathogen
soil pH
availability of food
competition between organisms

abiotic

biotic

B The diagram opposite shows part of a woodland food web.

There is an outbreak of a disease that kills only ladybirds. Use the food web to explain how this affects other organisms in the woodland.

Circle the correct **bold** word and complete each sentence.

a The number of ladybirds will **increase/decrease** because

_____

_____

b The number of aphids will **increase/decrease** because

_____

_____

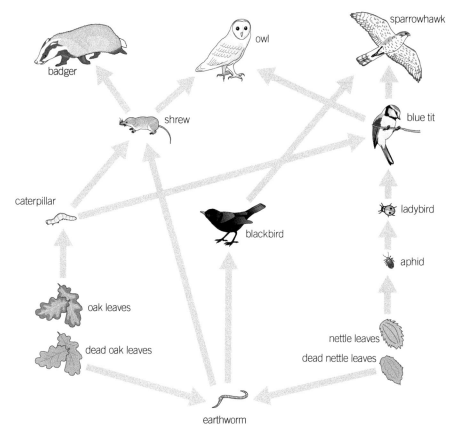

c The number of caterpillars will **increase/decrease** because

_____

_____

What you need to remember

Abiotic factors that may affect communities of organisms include: moisture levels, _____ intensity, wind intensity and direction, soil pH and _____ content, temperature, the _____ _____ level in the air for plants, and the availability of oxygen for aquatic animals. _____ factors that may affect communities of organisms include: availability of _____, new competitors, new predators arriving, and new pathogens.

A Scientists placed a line transect from the water's edge up to the top of a rocky shore.

They counted the number of barnacles and mussels found in a 0.25 m² area at different places along the transect. To do this they used the equipment shown opposite.

What is this equipment called?

_____

← 0.5 metre (internal dimension) →

wire or string   metal or wooden frame

B The scientists' results are shown below.

Distance from the water's edge in m	Number of mussels per 0.25 m²	Number of barnacles per 0.25 m²
0	0	0
5	6	0
10	18	0
15	12	9
20	7	16

What conclusions can be drawn from the data?

Tick the correct boxes.

W Mussels live in a drier environment than barnacles. ☐

X Mussels were more evenly distributed up the shore than barnacles. ☐

Y There were more mussels than barnacles in the area sampled. ☐

Z Neither muscles nor barnacles can live more than 20 m away from the water's edge. ☐

C Calculate an estimate for the number of barnacles per square metre living 15 m from the water's edge.

_____

What you need to remember

Scientists called _____ study the make-up of ecosystems. They look at how abiotic and _____ factors affect organisms. They study the _____ of organisms (how common they are) and their _____ (where they are). Ecologists also study the effect of changes in the environment on the organisms in a particular ecosystem.

_____ are used to estimate the population of plants in an area. A line _____ can be used to show how the distribution of organisms changes between two points.

B15.4 Competition in animals

A There is competition between organisms in an ecosystem.

Circle the resources that animals compete for.

light   **a mate**   **food**   **space to grow**   **territory**

B Foxes are omnivores. This means they eat a range of both plants and animals.

Using what you know about competition between animals, explain how this helps them to survive.

_____

_____

C Draw a line to match each animal adaptation to its function in competing with other animals.

Adaptation	Function
brightly coloured tail feathers	finding food
good eyesight	avoiding being eaten by predators
prickles	attracting a mate
living in a pack	maintaining a territory

What you need to remember

Animals compete with each other for food, territories, and a _____ (an organism to breed with). The best- _____ organisms are those most likely to win the competition for resources, so they will survive and reproduce to produce healthy _____.

There is competition between members of the same species and between members of _____ species.

B15.5 Competition in plants

A Plants compete with each other for resources.

Draw a line to match each resource plants compete for to its function in healthy plant growth.

Resource	Function
light	so their roots can take in enough water and minerals, and so their leaves can capture enough light
space to grow	to make the chemicals they need for growth
minerals from the soil	so they can keep their tissues rigid
water	so they can photosynthesise and make food

B Circle the correct **bold** words to complete the description of one way plants avoid competition.

Plants use seed **dispersal/pollination** to spread their seeds as far as possible. The seedlings will grow **away from/ close to** the parent plant and each other. This **increases/reduces** the competition between them for resources such as **light/food** and **mates/space**. This **decreases/increases** their chance of survival.

C A group of students carried out an investigation into the effect of competition on plants.

The bar charts opposite show their results.

- Write an **H** next to their hypothesis.
- Write a **C** next to their conclusion.
- Write an **E** next to their scientific explanation.

Note that one box should remain blank.

The seeds that were spread out grew the most.

Plant growth will be affected by how crowded they are.

It is important to keep all other conditions the same.

Plants that are close to each other have to compete more for resources.

What you need to remember

Plants _____ with each other for:

- light for photosynthesis, to make _____
- _____ for photosynthesis and for keeping their tissues rigid and supported
- nutrients (minerals) from the _____
- space to grow.

Plants have many _____ that make them good competitors.

B15.6 Adapt and survive

A Tick the boxes to show what resources each organism needs in order to survive.

The first column has been done for you.

	✓ if organism needs oxygen	✓ if organism needs water	✓ if organism needs carbon dioxide	✓ if organism needs food	✓ if organism needs light
yeast (microscopic fungus)	✓				
cactus (plant)					
shark (animal)	✓				

B Organisms that survive and reproduce in the most difficult conditions are known as extremophiles.

Draw a line to match each condition to the adaptation extremophiles have in order to survive there.

Condition

high salt concentration

high temperature

low temperature

Adaptation

enzymes that are resistant to denaturation

chemical in cells that acts like antifreeze

special cytoplasm in cells to stop water moving out by osmosis

C Circle **true** or **false** for each statement about adaptations.

a Animals need light in order to survive. **true/false**

b Some microorganisms can survive without oxygen. **true/false**

c Herbivores are animals that are adapted to eating other animals. **true/false**

d Only microorganisms can survive in extreme conditions. **true/false**

e Bacteria that can live in temperatures over 45 °C are known as thermophiles. **true/false**

What you need to remember

Organisms, including microorganisms, have features (_____) that enable them to survive in the conditions in which they normally live. _____ have adaptations that enable them to live in environments with extreme conditions of salt concentration, _____, or pressure.

B15.7 Adaptation in animals

A Adaptations in animals can be structural (what the animal looks like), behavioural (how the animal behaves), or functional (related to processes that happen inside the body).

Draw a line to match each adaptation to its type.

Adaptation		Type
migration to a warmer climate in the winter •		structural
thick fur for insulation •		
kidneys that produce very concentrated urine •		behavioural
sleeping in cool burrows during the day •		
camouflage •		functional

B Below is a list of adaptations seen in animals.

a Circle the adaptations of animals that live in hot climates.

b Underline the adaptations of animals that live in cold climates.

small surface area to volume ratio   **very little sweating**

layer of blubber under the skin   **thick fur coat**

active only in the early morning and evening **large surface area to volume ratio**

chemical that acts like antifreeze in cells   **large, thin ears**

C The picture opposite shows a fennec fox. It lives in the Sahara desert, North Africa.

a Describe **one** structural adaptation that helps it to survive the hot days.

_____

_____

_____

b Describe **one** structural adaptation that helps it to survive the cold nights.

_____

_____

_____

What you need to remember

Animals have adaptations that help them to get the resources they need to survive and reproduce. These include:

- _____ adaptations, for example camouflage or blubber for insulation
- behavioural adaptations, such as _____ to move to a better climate for the summer
- _____ adaptations related to processes such as reproduction and metabolism, for example, antifreeze in the cells of fish that live in cold water.

B15.8 Adaptation in plants

A Why do plants need water?

Tick all the correct boxes.

W to carry out respiration ☐

X to carry out photosynthesis ☐

Y to provide animals with food ☐

Z to keep their tissues rigid ☐

B Plants that live in very hot, dry conditions have to conserve water.

Choose the correct words to complete the paragraph that explains why.

oxygen	leaves	stomata	carbon dioxide	roots

adaptations	photosynthesis	evaporation	xylem

During the day plants use light to carry out _____ and produce food. This reaction takes place in the

_____ and requires _____ _____ . This gas travels into the leaves through tiny

holes called _____ . Water is lost by _____ when these holes are open. Therefore, plants that

live in very hot, dry conditions have _____ to conserve water.

C Cacti are plants that are adapted to live in hot, dry deserts.

Draw a line to match each cactus adaptation to its function.

Adaptation	Function
leaves are spines	reduces water loss
roots are spread over a wide area	so water is available at all times
stem stores water	increases uptake of water

What you need to remember

Plants have adaptations that enable them to survive in the conditions in which they normally live.

Common plant adaptations include:

- for plants that live in hot conditions, a low surface area to volume ratio to _____ water loss from leaves

- protection from herbivores, for example the sharp _____ on a cactus

- extensive _____ systems, to collect as much water as possible in dry conditions

- storing _____ in tissues, to use in periods of dry weather.

B15 Practice questions

01 A group of students was asked to estimate the number of dandelions on the school field.

Figure 1 shows the field.

15 m

7 m

Figure 1

01.1 Calculate the area of the field. [2 marks]

_____ m²

01.2 They decided to use a sample area called a quadrat. How should they use the quadrat in their investigation?

Tick **two** boxes. [2 marks]

S Place the quadrat where there are many dandelions. ☐

T Randomly place the quadrat. ☐

U Take fewer than five readings. ☐

V Take more than five readings. ☐

01.3 The results from the investigation are shown in **Table 1**.

Table 1

Quadrat number	Number of dandelions
1	0
2	1
3	3
4	0
5	2
6	1
7	3
8	1
9	1
10	2

What is the mode of the number of dandelions counted? [1 mark]

HINT The mode is the most popular number.

_____

01.4 Calculate the mean number of dandelions. Show your working out. [2 mark]

_____

01.5 The area of the quadrat is 0.25 m².

What calculation could the students use to estimate the number of dandelions in the field?

Tick **one** box. [1 mark]

W mean number of dandelions per quadrat × area of field in m² ☐

X (mean number of dandelions per quadrat × 4) × area of field in m² ☐

Y (area of field in m²/4) × mean number of dandelions per quadrat ☐

Z (area of quadrat in m²/4) × mean number of dandelions per quadrat ☐

B15 Checklist

	Student Book	☺	☺	☹
I can define the term stable community.	15.1			
I can describe how organisms are adapted to the conditions in which they live.	15.1			
I can explain the relationship between communities and ecosystems.	15.1			
I can name some of the factors that affect communities.	15.2			
I can describe how to measure the distribution of living things in their natural environment.	15.3			
I can calculate the mean, median, and mode of data.	15.3			
I can describe why animals compete.	15.4			
I can name the factors that animals are competing for in a habitat.	15.4			
I can describe how animals are adapted to the environment they live in.	15.4			
I can describe what makes an animal a successful competitor.	15.4			
I can explain what plants compete for.	15.5			
I can describe how plants compete.	15.5			
I can describe adaptations that plants have to make them successful competitors.	15.5			
I can identify what organisms need in order to survive.	15.6			
I can describe how organisms are adapted to survive in many different conditions.	15.6			
I can describe some of the ways in which animals are adapted in order to survive.	15.7			
I can suggest some of the ways in which plants are adapted in order to survive.	15.8			

B16.1 Feeding relationships

A Read the story below.

> Zara walked outside. It was a lovely, sunny day and the birch tree was swaying in the light breeze.
>
> A butterfly fluttered past and landed on the rose bush in the centre of the garden.
>
> Her cat, Milo, sauntered past, rubbing his fur against her legs.

a Draw a box around all the producers.

b Underline the consumers.

c Draw a star next to the primary consumer.

d Write a **C** next to the carnivore.

e Circle the predators.

B Use the names of the organisms below to complete the food chain.

    ladybird   **aphid**   **blue tit**   **tomato plant**   **hawk**

_____ → _____ → _____ → _____ → _____

C A population of rabbits lives in a field. Foxes are predators of rabbits.

Study the graph opposite.

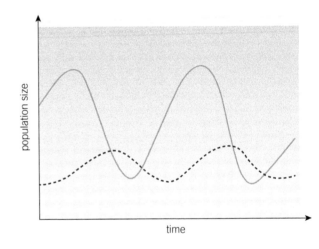

a Label the lines to show which represents the population of foxes and which represents the population of rabbits.

b Tick the boxes next to all the correct statements.

W As the number of rabbits goes up, the number of foxes goes down. ☐

X When the number of rabbits goes down, the amount of grass in the field decreases. ☐

Y As fox numbers increase, the population of rabbits decreases. ☐

Z As the number of rabbits increases, so does the number of foxes. ☐

What you need to remember

Photosynthetic organisms (green plants and _____) are the producers of biomass.

Feeding relationships can be represented by food chains. All food chains begin with a _____, which is eaten by primary _____. These may be eaten by secondary consumers, which may be eaten by _____ consumers.

Consumers that eat other animals (their prey) are _____. In a stable community the numbers of predators and prey rise and fall in cycles.

B16.2 Materials cycling

A Number the sentences in order to show one way in which mineral ions are recycled.

The first one has been done for you.

	The animal dies.
1	Plant material is eaten by an animal.
	Plants take up mineral ions through their roots.
	Mineral ions are released into the soil.
	Decomposers break down the dead body.

B Water is moved around by the water cycle.

Draw a line to match the name of each stage of the water cycle to its meaning.

Stage	Meaning
evaporation	loss of water from plant leaves
transpiration	water changes from a liquid into vapour
condensation	falling of liquid water to the surface of the Earth
precipitation	water changes from vapour into a liquid

C Label the diagram opposite, using the stages of the water cycle from activity **B** above.

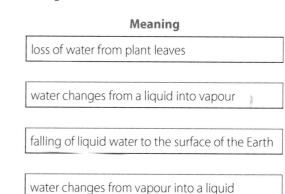
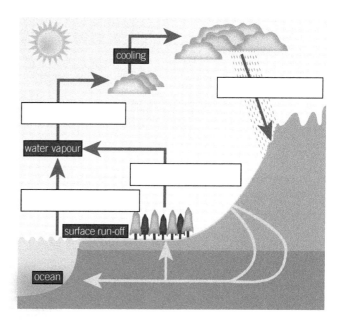

What you need to remember

Materials such as water and carbon are constantly recycled to provide resources for organisms. The

_____ of dead animals and plants by microorganisms returns mineral ions to the

_____ .

The water _____ describes how fresh water is available for plants and animals on land before

draining into the seas. Water is continuously evaporated, condensed, and _____ as rain or snow.

B16.3 The carbon cycle

A Here are some processes involved in the carbon cycle.

respiration   **combustion**   **photosynthesis**   **feeding**

For each statement below, choose the process it is describing. Write each process only once.

a glucose + oxygen → carbon dioxide + water   _____

b how carbon is passed from plants to animals   _____

c one way that carbon is taken from the air   _____

d the burning of fuels, which releases carbon dioxide into the air   _____

B Write the processes from activity **A** above on the diagram below to complete the carbon cycle.

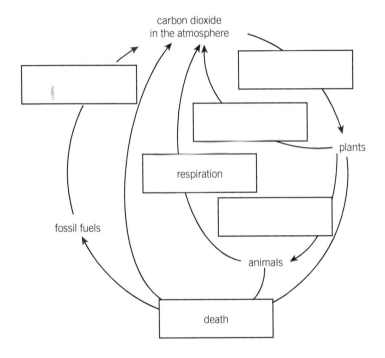

C The amount of carbon dioxide in the atmosphere remained fairly constant for millions of years.

Using the carbon cycle, explain why.

_____

_____

_____

_____

What you need to remember

Carbon is recycled by the carbon _____ . The burning of fossil _____ , respiration, and the _____ of dead plants and animals by microorganisms return carbon to the atmosphere as _____ _____ . Plants take up carbon dioxide during _____ . The carbon is stored in their tissues. The carbon is passed to animals when they _____ plants.

B16 Practice questions

01 Carbon is cycled between living things and the environment by the carbon cycle.
This is shown in **Figure 1**.

Figure 1

01.1 Which organism is a producer?
Tick **one** box. [1 mark]

T green plant ☐

U cow ☐

V microorganism ☐

01.2 Name the processes represented by **A**, **B**, and **C** in **Figure 1**. [3 marks]

A _____

B _____

C _____

01.3 Which word equation shows respiration?
Tick **one** box.

HINT Respiration is the reverse of photosynthesis. So if you know one equation, you also know the other.

W carbon dioxide + oxygen →
　　　　　　　　　　glucose + water ☐

X glucose + water →
　　　　　　　　　carbon dioxide + oxygen ☐

Y glucose + oxygen →
　　　　　　　　　carbon dioxide + water ☐

Z carbon dioxide + water →
　　　　　　　　　glucose + oxygen ☐

01.4 Explain the role of microorganisms in the carbon cycle. [2 marks]

_____

_____

_____

_____

01.5 In the Arctic, process **B** in **Figure 1** is much slower than in most other ecosystems.
Explain why. [2 marks]

_____

_____

_____

_____

_____

01.6 **Table 1** shows the mass of carbon dioxide moved by each process per year in billion tonnes.

Table 1

Process	Mass of carbon dioxide moved in billion tonnes
respiration	460
B	470
C	50

Explain the overall effect of the information in **Table 1** on the amount of carbon in the atmosphere. [4 marks]

HINT Calculate the mass of carbon dioxide removed from the atmosphere, and also the mass added.

_____

_____

_____

_____

_____

_____

_____

_____

B16 Checklist

	Student Book	☺	😐	☹
I can explain the importance of photosynthesis in feeding relationships.	16.1			
I can describe the main feeding relationships within a community.	16.1			
I can explain how the numbers of predators and prey in a community are related.	16.1			
I can describe how materials are recycled in a stable community.	16.2			
I can explain the importance of decay.	16.2			
I can describe what the carbon cycle is.	16.3			
I can name the processes that remove carbon dioxide from the atmosphere and return it again.	16.3			

B17.1 The human population explosion

A A forest has high biodiversity. What does this tell you about the forest?

Tick the correct box.

W It covers a large area. ☐

X It is home to a high population of one species. ☐

Y It is not a stable ecosystem. ☐

Z It contains a wide variety of different organisms. ☐

B Human activity can affect biodiversity.

For each activity, describe how it affects the biodiversity of the area.

a cutting down a natural tropical rainforest to form an oil palm plantation

_____

_____

b using chemical pesticides on farmland

_____

_____

C The graph opposite shows recorded and predicted human populations.

a Give the human population in 1960.

_____

b Describe how the graph predicts human population will change.

_____

_____

c Explain why these predictions may not be accurate.

_____

_____

What you need to remember

_____ is the variety of all the different species of organisms on Earth, or within an ecosystem.

Humans reduce the amount of land available for other animals and plants by building, quarrying, farming, and dumping _____.

The future of the human species on Earth relies on us maintaining a _____ level of biodiversity.

Many human activities are _____ biodiversity.

The human population is _____ rapidly. This means that more _____ are being used and more waste is produced.

B17.2 Land and water pollution

A Land and water can be polluted in many different ways.

Draw a line to match each human activity to the type of pollution it causes.

Human activity

| nuclear weapon testing |

| farming |

| household waste |

| human bodily waste |

Type of pollution

| toxic chemicals spreading from landfill sites |

| sewage |

| radioactive waste |

| pesticides in waterways |

B Number the sentences in order to show how fertilisers from farms can kill the life in a pond.

The first one has been done for you.

	Algae and water plants in the pond grow rapidly.
	The pond contains no life – it is 'dead'.
	Plants and algae die and are decayed by microorganisms that use oxygen from the water.
	Oxygen levels in the water fall rapidly – animals in the pond cannot survive.
1	Fertilisers are washed from the soil and enter the pond.

C A group of scientists measured the pH, oxygen, and nitrate levels in three different lakes. Their data is shown below.

Which lake is each statement describing?

Write the letter of the lake in the space.

a can support a high level of biodiversity

_____

Lake	pH	Oxygen level	Nitrate level
X	6.5	normal	normal
Y	7.2	high	low
Z	7.9	low	high

b is polluted with fertilisers _____

c has an acidic pH _____

d is most likely to have the lowest level of biodiversity _____

What you need to remember

If waste is not handled properly it may pollute the land and water. Pollution can occur on land from landfill and from toxic _____ such as pesticides and herbicides. These may also be washed from land to _____ .

Pollution can occur in water from sewage, _____ (which are used to increase plant growth), or toxic chemicals.

Pollution kills plants and animals, which can _____ biodiversity.

B17.3 Air pollution

A Fill in the missing words.

a Cars are now fitted with catalytic _____ , which remove polluting gases from exhaust fumes.

b Acid rain has a pH of _____ than 7.

c Global _____ is caused by smoke particles reflecting sunlight so less hits the surface of the Earth.

B Name the following:

a The haze of smoke particles and acidic gases that is common in some cities.

   _____

b An acidic gas formed when fuels are burnt. Its formula is CO_2.

   _____

c The tiny solid particles found in smoke.

   _____

d The organ that is damaged by breathing in smoke.

   _____

e An acidic gas that causes breathing problems in people. Its formula is SO_2.

   _____

f Fuels, including coal and oil, that release acidic gases when burnt.

   _____

What you need to remember

Pollution can occur in the _____ from smoke and from acidic gases. When fossil _____ are burnt, acidic gases are formed that dissolve in rainwater to form acid _____ . Acid rain damages the environment. It can kill trees and make lakes and streams acidic.

Smoke pollution causes an increase in tiny particulates in the air, which can cause global _____ and affect human health.

B17.4 Deforestation and peat destruction

A Write down:

a **one** reason why deforestation decreases biodiversity

1 _____

b **two** reasons why deforestation increases the amount of carbon dioxide in the atmosphere

1 _____

2 _____

c **three** reasons why deforestation is being carried out.

1 _____

2 _____

3 _____

B In 1970 there were an estimated 4 100 000 km² of rainforest in Brazil.

In 2015 this area was estimated to be 3 331 065 km².

a Calculate the estimated area of forest lost in Brazil between 1970 and 2015.

_____ km²

b Calculate the percentage of forest lost during this time.

_____ %

C Circle **true** or **false** for each statement about peat.

a Peat is made from plant material that has decayed completely.   **true/false**

b Peat bogs have acidic conditions.   **true/false**

c Because of the conditions, peat bogs are not home to plants or animals.   **true/false**

d Peat can be used as a fuel.   **true/false**

e Peat is a non-renewable resource.   **true/false**

What you need to remember

Deforestation is the removal of _____ without replacing them. Large-scale deforestation is used to provide land for farming and to grow crops for biofuels.

Peat is made of plant material that has not completely _____ . The destruction of peat bogs to produce garden compost _____ biodiversity in this habitat. The decay or burning of peat releases _____ _____ into the atmosphere.

B17.5 Global warming

A Since the 1950s the amount of carbon dioxide in the atmosphere has been measured in Hawaii.

The graph opposite shows the data.

a Describe the trend in the data.

_____

_____

b Suggest **one** reason for this trend.

_____

_____

_____

Atmospheric CO_2 at
Mauna Loa observatory

B The diagram opposite shows the greenhouse effect.

Write letters in the boxes to show where each statement belongs on the diagram.

☐ energy transferred from the Sun

☐ energy absorbed by greenhouse gases in the atmosphere

☐ energy reflected and transferred into space

☐ energy reradiated back to Earth

C Draw a line to match each change brought about by global warming to its biological impact.

Change	Biological impact
rising sea levels	animals migrate at different times of the year
change in seasons	the distribution of plants will change
less rain in some areas	populations of animals adapted to cold climates will reduce
increase in Arctic temperatures	loss of biodiversity in low-lying areas

What you need to remember

Because of human activity, levels of carbon dioxide and _____ in the atmosphere are increasing. This is contributing to global _____ .

Consequences of global warming include:

* loss of habitat when low-lying areas are flooded by rising _____ levels
* changes in the distribution of species in areas where temperature or rainfall has changed
* changes to the _____ patterns of animals.

B17.6 Maintaining biodiversity

A Many zoos carry out breeding programmes. They breed endangered animals to increase their population in the hope that they can be released back to the wild.

There are benefits and drawbacks of breeding programmes in zoos.

For each statement, put a ✗ if it is a drawback and a ✓ if it is a benefit.

W Inbreeding may occur. ☐

X Zoos educate the public. ☐

Y Zoos may be the only protected habitat for some animals. ☐

Z Animals are kept in captivity. ☐

B Read the information below about landfill sites.

> Both household and industrial waste are taken to landfill sites to be buried in the ground.
>
> To build landfill sites large areas of land have to be cleared. This could be waste ground or it could be land that is habitat to many plants and animals.
>
> When the rubbish is in the ground some chemicals can leak out of the rubbish and enter the land or waterways.
>
> When the landfill site is full of rubbish, it can be covered in soil and planted with trees and bushes.

a Underline the section that describes how landfill sites could reduce biodiversity.

b Circle the section that explains how landfill sites can cause pollution.

c Give **one** way in which people can reduce the amount of rubbish that goes to landfills.

C Study the data in the chart opposite.

Describe what the chart shows.

_____

_____

_____

_____

_____

_____

What you need to remember

Scientists and concerned citizens have put programmes in place to reduce the negative effects of humans on ecosystems and biodiversity.

These include _____ programmes for endangered species, protection and regeneration of rare habitats, the reintroduction of field margins and _____ , the reduction of deforestation, and recycling _____ .

B17 Practice questions

01 Burning fossil fuels releases polluting gases into the atmosphere.

Draw a line from each polluting gas to the environmental effect it causes. [2 marks]

Polluting gas

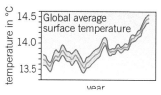

| carbon dioxide |

| sulfur dioxide |

Environmental effect

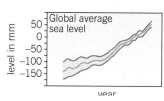

| hole in the ozone layer |

| global warming |

| acid rain |

02 The graphs in **Figure 1** were published by the IPCC (Intergovernmental Panel on Climate Change).

Global average surface temperature

Global average sea level

Figure 1

02.1 Describe the correlation between global average surface temperature and sea level. [1 mark]

HINT A correlation is a relationship: there is a link between the variables.

02.2 Suggest **one** explanation for this relationship. [2 marks]

02.3 Explain how this change in sea level could affect biodiversity. [3 marks]

03 A group of students was asked to carry out an investigation into the effects of acid rain on living organisms.

They chose to investigate the hypothesis 'The more concentrated the acid rain, the fewer seeds will germinate.'

They used the following method.

1. Line five Petri dishes with cotton wool.

2. Place three cress seeds in each dish.

3. Every day, add water or sulfuric acid to the dishes. Use a different solution in each dish:
   - distilled water (0 g/dm³ sulfuric acid)
   - 10 g/dm³ sulfuric acid
   - 25 g/dm³ sulfuric acid
   - 50 g/dm³ sulfuric acid
   - 100 g/dm³ sulfuric acid.

4. After a week, count how many seeds have germinated. Calculate this as a percentage.

03.1 Describe how the method could be improved to produce more valid results. [4 marks]

HINT Look at whether they used control variables. Also, think about how many seeds they used.

03.2 After improving their method, the students carried out the investigation. **Table 1** shows their results.

Table 1

Concentration of sulfuric acid in g/dm³	Percentage of seeds that had germinated
0	92%
10	87%
25	62%
50	30%
100	5%

Plot this data as a line graph. [3 marks]

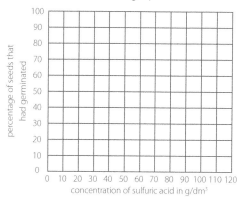

03.3 Explain if the data supports their hypothesis or not. [2 marks]

B17 Checklist

	Student Book	☺	😐	☹
I can define biodiversity and explain why it is important.	17.1			
I can name some of the effects of the growth in human population on the Earth and its resources.	17.1			
I can describe how human activities pollute the land.	17.2			
I can describe how human activities pollute the water.	17.2			
I can describe how acid rain is formed.	17.3			
I can explain how acid rain affects living organisms.	17.3			
I can describe how air pollution causes global dimming and smog.	17.3			
I can define deforestation.	17.4			
I can explain why loss of biodiversity matters.	17.4			
I can describe the environmental effects of destroying peat bogs.	17.4			
I can define global warming.	17.5			
I can explain how global warming could affect life on Earth.	17.5			
I can describe how waste, deforestation, and global warming all have an impact on biodiversity.	17.6			
I can describe some of the ways people are trying to reduce the impact of human activities on ecosystems and maintain biodiversity.	17.6			

Answers

B1.1

A slide – **Y**
   objective lens – **X**
   eyepiece lens – **W**
   light – **Z**
B a true
   b false
   c true
   d false
C $\frac{10}{100} = 0.1$ mm (or 100 μm)

What you need to remember
magnify, small, electrons, magnification, resolution / resolving power, larger / bigger, more

B1.2

A nucleus – contains genes that carry the instructions for making proteins
   cell membrane – controls the passage of substances into and out of the cell
   ribosomes – where proteins are made
   mitochondria – where aerobic respiration takes place, which releases energy
   cytoplasm – where most of the chemical reactions in the cell take place
B from top: cell membrane, ribosomes, mitochondria, cytoplasm, nucleus
C nucleus – in both types of cell
   chloroplast – only in plant cells
   mitochondria – in both types of cell
   cell membrane – in both types of cell

What you need to remember
nucleus, cytoplasm, membrane, energy, proteins, wall, chloroplasts, vacuole

B1.3

A animal sperm cell – underline
   MRSA bacteria – circle
   cold virus – neither
   yeast cell – underline
   E. coli bacteria – circle
   root hair cell – underline
B a plasmid
   b flagella
   c cytoplasm
   d cell wall, slime capsule
C $\frac{1}{1000} = 0.1$ mm

   $\frac{1}{1000} = 0.001$ m

What you need to remember
eukaryotic, nucleus, prokaryotic, nucleus, plasmids

B1.4

A X
B nerve cell – carries electrical impulses around the body
   muscle cell – contracts and relaxes to help movement

sperm cell – contains genetic information from the male parent
C a tail
   b energy (to the tail)
   c break down the outer layers of the egg
   d genes / genetic information from the father

What you need to remember
differentiate, specialised, function, nerve, muscle, egg

B1.5

A left to right: root hair cell, xylem cell, phloem cell
B phloem cell – sieve plates – allows dissolved food to move up and down the stem
   xylem cell – rings of lignin – helps withstand the pressure of water
   root hair cell – increased surface area – increases the amount of water that the plant can absorb
C a false
   b true
   c false
   d true

What you need to remember
specialised, area, water, lignin, sieve

B1.6

A gas, solute
   net
   higher, concentration
   random
B **S, Q, P, R**
C increase in air temperature – rate increases
   blood moving more quickly – rate increases
   make the lungs smaller – rate decreases
   more oxygen in the air – rate increases

What you need to remember
movement, higher, lower, rate, gradient, area, oxygen

B1.7

A water, concentrated, partially, membrane
B arrow from left to right
C **X** – 0.5 – 0.1 – **solution is hypotonic**
   Y – 0.8 – 1.2 – **solution is hypertonic**
   Z – 0.4 – 0.4 – **solution is isotonic**
D cell **X** – cell would swell up and burst
   cell **Y** – cell would become shrivelled

What you need to remember
diffusion, water, concentrated, membrane, water, same, hypertonic, hypotonic

B1.8

A top diagram – turgid (normal)
   middle diagram – flaccid
   bottom diagram – plasmolysed
B a curved line of best fit drawn
   b (80, −20)
C increased, into, decreased, out of, 30, the same as

What you need to remember
turgor, loses, flaccid, membrane, plasmolysis

B1.9

A Active transport moves substances from – a more dilute solution to a more concentrated solution.
   Cells involved in active transport normally have – many mitochondria for energy release.
   One use of active transport is for the movement of – glucose from the gut into the bloodstream.
   Active transport moves substances against – the concentration gradient.
B Y
C as the rate of respiration increases, so does the rate of active transport

What you need to remember
dilute, gradient, respiration, root, soil, higher

B1.10

A **X** – 2 – 4 – **24** – 8 – 3:1
   Y – 4 – **16** – 96 – **64** – 1.5:1
B smaller, exchange, gases, diffusion, waste
C one from: large surface area, good blood supply, thin walls

What you need to remember
large, decreases, large, thin, blood, fish

B1 Practice questions

01.1 **Z** [1]
01.2 $= 4 \times 10$ [1]
      $= \times 40$ [1]
02.1 osmosis [1]
02.2 cut up plant tissue (e.g., potato) into pieces of a similar mass and shape; [1] measure the mass of each one using balances / scales; [1] submerge each in a different concentration of sugar solution; [1] leave for a specified time (e.g., 30 minutes); [1] remove plant tissue and dry; [1] measure the mass and calculate mass change [1]
03.1 root hair cell [1]
03.2 has projection (hair), [1] which increases surface area [1] to increase uptake of water (and mineral ions) [1]

B2.1

A   gene – a small piece of DNA that controls a characteristic
cell – what living organisms are made up of
chromosome – a string of many genes
nucleus – part of the cell where genetic material is found

B   a   true
b   false
c   false
d   true

C   W, Y, Z

What you need to remember
cycle, two, mitosis, repair

B2.2

A   Embryos contain stem cells, which are – unspecialised.
Stem cells can become – any type of cell.
Most adult cells are – specialised.
During the process of differentiation – genes are switched on or off.

B   contains stem cells – both plants and animals
growth happens throughout life – plants only
differentiation is permanent – both plants and animals
stem cells are found in several different places – animals only
stem cells are found only in regions called meristems – plants only

C   tip of a root

What you need to remember
differentiate, embryos, meristems, root

B2.3

A   T
B   W, Y
C   one from: could be used to save some rare plants from extinction; provides a way of producing large populations of identical plants for research; enables production of large numbers of plants for sale; produces large numbers of identical crop plants with special features, such as disease resistance

What you need to remember
adult, diabetes, meristems, quickly

B2.4

A   from top: X, Z, W, V, Y
B   a   blue circle – the potential of stem cells to treat conditions such as paralysis and diabetes
b   red circle – there is some concern that using embryonic stem cells to treat people might cause cancer
c   box – the embryos will be destroyed after being used
d   underline – some people feel that this money would be better spent on research into other areas of medicine.

What you need to remember
risks, ethical, therapeutic, reject, adult

B2 Practice questions

01   nucleus, genes, DNA, pairs of [2]
02.1   A [1]
02.2   the number of chromosomes doubles [1]
03.1   X [1]
03.2   one from: paralysis, Type 1 diabetes [1]
03.3   two from: can differentiate into any cell, will not be rejected by the patient, can divide and grow rapidly [2]
03.4   one from: the embryo is a potential new life / has a right to life; once the cells are removed, the embryo is destroyed [1]

B3.1

A   cells → tissues → organs → organ systems → whole body
B   muscular – helps churn the food and digestive juices together
glandular – produces digestive juices that break down food
epithelial – covers the inside and outside of the organ
C   system X – reproductive
system Y – circulatory
system Z – skeletal

What you need to remember
cells, muscle, tissues, stomach, glandular, systems, digestive

B3.2

A   clockwise from top: gullet, stomach, large intestine, small intestine, liver
B   a   anus
b   large
c   stomach
d   pancreas
e   gullet / oesophagus
f   mouth
g   liver
h   small

What you need to remember
digestive, organs, insoluble, small, bloodstream

B3.3

A   carbohydrates – pasta – **provide energy**
lipids – olive oil – **provide energy, building new cell membranes and hormones**
protein – meat / fish / nuts / dairy products / pulses / eggs / tofu – forming new tissues, enzymes, and hormones
B   left to right: lipid, glucose, amino acid, protein
C   starch – orange iodine solution – blue-black colour
simple sugar (e.g., glucose) – blue Benedict's solution – brick-red colour
protein – blue Biuret solution – purple colour

lipid – ethanol – cloudy, white layer

What you need to remember
proteins, starch / glycogen / cellulose, glycerol, amino

B3.4

A   a substance that increases the rate of a chemical reaction
B   substrate, active, lock and key, products, enzyme
C   mass of catalyst – control variable
volume of hydrogen peroxide – control variable
volume of gas produced over time – dependent variable
temperature of catalyst – control variable
type of catalyst – independent variable

What you need to remember
catalysts, rate, amino, active, substrate, key, metabolism, small, breaking

B3.5

A   S, T, V
B   0, 37, 37, 37, 41
C   W

What you need to remember
temperature, optimum, denature, active, substrate

B3.6

A   X, Y, Z
B   protein – protease
lipid – lipase
starch – amylase
C   a   true
b   true
c   false
d   true

What you need to remember
glands, insoluble, Enzymes, protein, lipases, lipids

B3.7

A   a   1.5 – 0.5 = 1.0
b   pepsin works best in acidic conditions
B   X, Y

What you need to remember
acid, low, alkaline, liver, gall bladder, duct, neutralise, small

B3 Practice questions

01.1   the mixture would no longer go blue-black / would stay orange [1]
01.2   get someone else to repeat the experiment using the same method; [1] compare the two sets of results [1]
01.3   y-axis labelled as 'time taken for all the starch to be digested in seconds'; [1] points correctly plotted; [2] line of best fit drawn [1]

01.4 amylase works best around pH 7 / optimum pH is around 7; [1] at pH below and above 7 the rate of reaction is slow [1]

02 anticlockwise from top: liver, gall bladder, pancreas [3]

B4.1

A plasma – transports all of the blood cells and other substances around the body
red blood cells – pick up oxygen from the lungs and carry it to all the body cells
white blood cells – form part of the body's defence system against harmful microorganisms
platelets – help the blood to clot at the site of a wound

B clockwise from bottom left: platelets, plasma, white blood cell, red blood cell

C They contain the red pigment haemoglobin – to pick up oxygen.
They have no nucleus – making more space for haemoglobin.
They are biconcave discs (pushed in on both sides) – giving them an increased surface area to volume ratio for diffusion.
They are very flexible – to fit through narrow blood vessels.

What you need to remember

heart, Plasma, haemoglobin, lungs, (harmful) microorganisms / pathogens, clotting

B4.2

A left to right: artery, vein, capillary

B T

C **U** – capillaries
V – vein
W – artery
X – capillaries
Y – vein
Z – artery

What you need to remember

veins, capillaries, valves, Humans, double, lungs

B4.3

A a circle – pulmonary vein
b box – pulmonary artery
c underline – vena cava
d triangle – aorta

B **U, S, Q, R, T, P**

C heart, fatty, oxygen, attack, stent, bypass, statins

What you need to remember

blood, two, ventricle, lungs, left, valves, oxygen, stents, heart, statins

B4.4

A **X, Z**

B a red underline – many people die before they can have their transplant
b blue underline – These are expensive to make
c green underline – The heart comes from a person who has died

C a 188 700 – 121 300 = 67 400
b $\dfrac{67\,400}{121\,300} \times 100 = 55.6\%$

What you need to remember

mechanical, animals, atrium, pacemaker, Artificial, Artificial

B4.5

A clockwise from left: lungs, trachea, bronchi, bronchiole, alveoli

B **W, Y**

C carbon dioxide – **0.04 – 4**
nitrogen – **80 – 80**
oxygen – **20 – 16**

What you need to remember

ribs, diaphragm, trachea, area, capillaries, oxygen, blood

B4.6

A **S** – flower – used for reproduction
T – leaf – where photosynthesis is carried out
U – stem – supports the leaves and flowers
V – roots – take up water and mineral ions

B anticlockwise from top: upper epidermis, palisade mesophyll, spongy mesophyll, lower epidermis, guard cell, stomata, air space, vascular bundle

C **X, Y, Z**

What you need to remember

roots, photosynthesis, epidermis, stomata, stem

B4.7

A water – carried in the xylem, moved from roots to leaves
mineral ions – carried in the xylem, moved from roots to leaves
sugars – carried in the phloem, moved from leaves to the rest of the plant

B **Y**

C a true
b true
c false
d true
e false

What you need to remember

Xylem, roots, leaves, Phloem, energy, protein / amino acids

B4.8

A water vapour – diffused out of the leaf
oxygen – diffused out of the leaf

carbon dioxide – diffused into the leaf

B **Q, P, T, S, R**

C a $\dfrac{1}{0.05} = 20$
$20 \times 6 = 120$
b $120 \times 70 = 8400$

What you need to remember

transpiration, leaf, guard, carbon dioxide, water, xylem

B4.9

A **R, T, U**

B **Y**

C 1 as the light intensity increases, the rate of transpiration increases
2 the rate of transpiration is higher in windy air than still air

What you need to remember

increase, carbon dioxide, water vapour, light, temperature, potometer, faster

B4 Practice questions

01.1 to carry oxygen [1] from the lungs to the body cells [1]

01.2 $5 \times \dfrac{45}{100}$ [1] = 2.25 (dm³) [1]

02.1 **Y** [1]

02.2 its diameter is only slightly bigger than that of the red blood cell [1]

02.3 $\dfrac{1}{1.4} = 0.7$ mm/s [3]

B5.1

A measles, tuberculosis

B stress – depression
diet – obesity
smoking – lung cancer
poor water quality – diarrhoea-linked diseases

C graph is a straight line showing a positive relationship (line extending upwards from the y-axis)

What you need to remember

mental, infectious, microorganism / pathogens, non-communicable, diet

B5.2

A a true
b false
c false
d true

B **R, Q, P, S**

C divide, fission, toxins, cells, headache

D common cold – air
cholera – water
chlamydia – direct contact

What you need to remember

microorganisms, viruses, toxins, viruses, air

B5.3

A   observation – The pregnant women delivered by doctors rather than midwives were much more likely to die of a fever.

hypothesis – Doctors are carring the cause of disease on their hands.

method – Make doctors wash their hands.

results – The number of deaths decreased.

conclusion – The hypothesis is correct, but the cause of death is not known.

B   T

C   malaria **Y**
measles **Z**
common cold **V**
Salmonella (food poisoning) **W**
Ebola **X**

What you need to remember

pathogens / microorganisms, spread, washing, vectors

B5.4

A   measles **V, 1**
HIV/AIDS **T, 2**
tobacco mosaic virus **U, 3**

B   **W, Z**

C   a   true
b   false
c   true
d   true

What you need to remember

measles, vaccine, immune / white blood, AIDS, blood, mosaic, vectors, photosynthesis

B5.5

A   *Salmonella* – vomiting and diarrhoea
gonorrhoea – discharge from vagina or penis
Agrobacterium tumefaciens infection – mass of cells on the shoot (crown gall)

B   raw
fridge
do not
after
whole chicken

C   Y

What you need to remember

bacteria, toxins, vaccinated, sexually, penis, antibiotics, condoms, plants, cells

B5.6

A   a   circle – rose black spot, athlete's foot, stem rust
b   underline – malaria

B   **X**

C   Insecticides are used in homes and offices to kill adult mosquitoes
Insect nets over beds – prevent mosquitoes biting people at night.

Antimalarial drugs – kill the protists in the blood.
Areas of standing water are drained to – remove mosquito larvae.

What you need to remember

fungi, photosynthesis, malaria, liver, nets, blood

B5.7

A   circle – stomach, skin, nose

B   producing antibodies – middle diagram
producing antitoxins – bottom diagram
ingesting pathogens – top diagram

C   **X, Z**

What you need to remember

barrier, platelets, trachea, mucus, cilia, acid, food, blood, antibodies

B5 Practice questions

01.1   malaria – protist
HIV/AIDS – virus
crown gall disease – bacteria
rose black spot – fungi [3 marks – all correct; 2 marks – 2 correct; 1 mark – 1 correct]

01.2   HIV/AIDS [1]

02.1   **Y** [1]

02.2   independent variable: treatment [1]
dependent variable: diameter of sores after 30 days of treatment [1]

02.3   it was a placebo / control [1] to check that the antibiotics helped reduce the size of the sores [1]

02.4   antibiotic **B** [1] because it reduced the diameter of the sore the most; [1] antibiotic **B** killed the bacteria / cured the infection most effectively [1]

B6.1

A   vaccine – contains dead or inactivated forms of a pathogen
immune – protected against a disease because of the action of white blood cells
antibody – a protein made by white blood cells that binds to a specific pathogen
antigens – unique proteins on the surface of a cell
pathogen – a microorganism that causes disease

B   **T, P, S, U, V, R, Q**

C   **W, Y**

What you need to remember

antigens, vaccine, antibodies, white, herd

B6.2

A   a   underline – aspirin, paracetamol, ibuprofen
b   circle – penicillin

B   a   false
b   true
c   false
d   true

C   grazed knee – antiseptic
migraine – painkiller
bacterial lung infection – antibiotic
common cold – painkiller
sprained ankle – painkiller
bacterial blood infection – antibiotic

D   **Z**

What you need to remember

painkillers, Antibiotics, resistant, viruses, cells

B6.3

A   aspirin – willow tree
digitalis – foxglove plant
penicillin – mould

B   **X**

C   a   yes
b   no
c   yes
d   yes

What you need to remember

plants, fungi / mould, antibiotic, Fleming

B6.4

A   A low dose of the drug is given to healthy volunteers – to check for side effects.
The drug is tested on cells in the laboratory – to check it is not toxic to living cells.
The drug is given to a small number of patients – to check if it treats the disease.
The drug is tested on live animals – to check it works in whole living organisms.
The drug is given to many patients – to find the optimum dose.

B   **Q, S, P, R, T**

C   randomly, placebo, doctor, double-blind, more, effective

What you need to remember

years, safe, animals, trials, dose, blind, placebo, doctor

B6 Practice questions

01.1   **X, Y** [2]

01.2   vaccine contains dead / inactive pathogens / viruses; [1] white blood cells produce antibodies; [1] memory cells 'remember' the antibody; [1] if body is infected with live virus, antibodies are made quickly [1]

01.3   the percentage increased [1]

01.4 $7.8 \times \dfrac{64}{100}$ [1]
= 4.992 [1]
= 5 million (people) [1]

01.5 the virus is not able to infect as many people [1] so it does not spread in the population [1]

B7.1

A your age – things you cannot change
lack of exercise – lifestyle choices
UV light from the sun – effects of the environment
radioactive substances in the air – effects of the environment
using sunbeds – lifestyle choices
drinking alcohol – lifestyle choices
your genes – things you cannot change
overeating – lifestyle choices

B   a   P
     b   R
     c   Q, S

C   W

What you need to remember
passed, Risk, increased, diabetes, causal, lung

B7.2

A normal cells – paler cells either side of central section
tumour cells – darker cells in centre of diagram

B produced by uncontrolled cell division – benign, malignant
can be life-threatening – benign, malignant
spread around the body – malignant
cells are contained in one place – benign
also known as cancer – malignant
can form secondary tumours – malignant

C lung cancer – tar in tobacco smoke
breast cancer – genetics
skin cancer – UV light
cervical cancer – virus infection

What you need to remember
cell, Benign, Malignant, secondary, UV, radiation, chemotherapy

B7.3

A shortage of oxygen in the blood – carbon monoxide
increase in heart rate – nicotine
breakdown in alveoli – tar
low birthweight – carbon monoxide
lung cancer – tar
stillbirth – carbon monoxide
throat cancer – tar
COPD – tar

B W, Y

C correlation, causal mechanism, nicotine, clot formation, an increase

What you need to remember
nicotine, monoxide, tar, heart, lung, bronchitis, oxygen, birthweight

B7.4

A circle – type 2 diabetes, heart disease

B Exercise increases muscle tissue – which increases metabolic rate.
Exercise lowers blood cholesterol levels – which reduces the risk of fatty deposits building on arteries.
People who exercise are less likely to become obese – which lowers the risk of developing type 2 diabetes.

C in both men and women, the higher a person's BMI index, the higher their risk of developing type 2 diabetes
overweight and obese women have a higher risk than men of the same BMI

What you need to remember
overweight, diabetes, blood, exercise, fatty, heart

B7.5

A top to bottom: feeling relaxed and happy, difficulty walking and talking, unconsciousness, death

B X, Y

C tar (from smoking) – chemical
UV light – ionising radiation
X-rays – ionising radiation
alcohol – chemical
radon gas – ionising radiation

What you need to remember
nervous, slows, coma, liver, pregnant, mutations, Sun, skin

B7 Practice questions

01.1 a group of cells that are dividing rapidly [2]
01.2 a disease that cannot be passed from person to person [1]
02.1 X, Y [2]
02.2 one from: the patient may not tell the truth, the patient may not be monitoring how much they smoke and drink [1]
02.3 D, A, B, E, C [2]
02.4 one from: heart disease, COPD, emphysema, bronchitis [1]

B8.1

A   **light**
carbon dioxide + **water** → glucose + **oxygen**
$6CO_2$ + $6H_2O$ → $C_6H_{12}O_6$ + $6O_2$

B a underline – she observed bubbles
   b circle – She placed a glowing splint to the test tube and it relit

C broad shape – big surface area for light to fall on
thin – diffusion distances for gases are short
stomata – to allow carbon dioxide to enter the leaf and oxygen to leave
veins – to bring water to the cells
air spaces – allow carbon dioxide to get to cells and oxygen to leave, by diffusion

What you need to remember
endothermic, algae, light, water, chlorophyll, glucose

B8.2

A temperature of water – control variable
distance of light to plant – independent variable
type of plant – control variable
volume of oxygen produced after 5 minutes – dependent variable
temperature of room – control variable
concentration of carbon dioxide in the water – control variable

B X

C X, Y

What you need to remember
light, carbon dioxide, limiting, brighter, increases, enzymes, increase

B8.3

A 1 Boil the leaf in ethanol to – remove the green colour.
   2 Rinse the leaf in hot water to – soften the leaf.
   3 Add iodine to the leaf to – test for starch.

B a fruit and tuber
   b tuber and seed
   c seed

C a true
   b false
   c true
   d true
   e false

What you need to remember
respiration, starch, cellulose, nitrate, proteins

B8 Practice questions

01.1 W [1]
01.2 the beaker of water absorbs the heat from the lamp [1]
01.3 8.2 + 8.4 = 16.6 [1]
$\frac{16.6}{2} = 8.3$ [1]
01.4 it increased [1]
01.5 the plant was carrying out photosynthesis [1] and removing carbon dioxide from the water [1]
01.6 as the distance of the lamp from the pondweed increased, the pH of the water increased by less; [1] the plant was carrying out photosynthesis at a slower rate; [1] and was not removing so much carbon dioxide from the water [1]

B9.1

A carbon dioxide – product
oxygen – reactant
water – product
glucose – reactant

B mitochondria / mitochondrion – small dark shape within cell

C   a   to contract, in order to move
    b   for active transport, to move mineral ions from the soil into the plant

What you need to remember

exothermic, oxygen, carbon dioxide, mitochondria, energy

B9.2

A   faster, increases, dilate, oxygenated, increases, deeply, oxygen, carbon dioxide

B   Z

C   increased, 70, Ruby, largest

What you need to remember

muscles, heart, glycogen, blood, oxygen, carbon dioxide

B9.3

A   X

B   Glucose is a reactant – aerobic respiration, anaerobic respiration
Oxygen is a reactant – aerobic respiration
Carbon dioxide is produced – aerobic respiration
Energy is transferred to the environment – aerobic respiration, anaerobic respiration
Cells can carry it out continuously – aerobic respiration

C   a   true
    b   false
    c   true
    d   true

What you need to remember

oxygen, lactic, less, oxygen, plant, ethanol

B9.4

A   W

B $C_6H_{12}O_6 + 6O_2 \rightarrow 6H_2O + 6CO_2$ – respiration
sucrose $\rightarrow$ glucose + fructose – breakdown of molecules
$6H_2O + 6CO_2 \rightarrow C_6H_{12}O_6 + 6O_2$ – photosynthesis
amino acids $\rightarrow$ protein – formation of molecules

C   proteins, liver, urea

What you need to remember

reactions, respiration, glucose, amino, urea, liver

B9 Practice questions

01.1   glucose $\rightarrow$ **ethanol** + carbon dioxide [1]

01.2   one from: making alcoholic drinks, making bread, making ethanol to use as a fuel [1]

01.3.1   one from: glucose is a reactant, energy is transferred, takes place in mitochondria, carbon dioxide is produced [1]

01.3.2   in animals lactic acid is produced; in yeast ethanol and carbon dioxide are produced [1]

02.1   change the temperature of the yeast [1] by placing the flask in a water bath at different temperatures; [1] measure the volume of gas (carbon dioxide) produced using the gas syringe; [1] measure gas produced over a certain time **or** time how long it takes to produce a certain volume of gas [1]

02.2   between 20 °C and around 37 °C the rate increased as the temperature increased; [1] between around 37 °C and 42 °C the rate stayed around constant; [1] between around 42 °C and 50 °C the rate decreased as the temperature increased [1]

B10.1

A   V, X, Y

B   a   increases
    b   decreases
    c   decreases
        as his temperature rises his skin produces sweat to help cool him down; sweat contains water

C   receptor – cells that detect stimuli (changes in the environment)
coordination centre – receives and processes information
effector – muscles or glands that bring about a response

What you need to remember

internal, glucose, hormonal, receptors

B10.2

A   from top:
eye – light
ear – sound, change in position
nose – chemical
skin – change in temperature, pressure, pain

B   eyes, impulse, neurone, brain, motor, muscles

C   X, Y

What you need to remember

electrical / nervous, stimuli, sensory, spinal, motor, muscles

B10.3

A   L, M, O

B   R, P, T, Q, S

D   a sensory neurone **W**
a motor neurone **V**
a relay neurone **U**
a receptor **Y**
an effector **X**
a synapse **Z**

What you need to remember

automatic, brain, harm, relay, effector, synapses, chemicals

B10 Practice questions

01   **X, Y** [2]

02.1   sensory [1]

02.2   motor [1]

02.3   arrow from left to right for neurone **A** [1]
arrow from left to right for neurone **B** [1]

03.1 $\frac{3}{120}$ [1] = 0.025 (seconds) [1]

03.2   to bring about a quick response, [1] to avoid harm [1]

04.1   synapse [1]

04.2   chemicals are released from neurone **C**; [1] they diffuse across the gap / synapse; [1] they bind with receptors on neurone **D** [1]

B11.1

A   R – pituitary gland – FSH
S – thyroid gland – thyroxine
T – adrenal gland – adrenaline
U – pancreas – insulin
V – ovary (female) – oestrogen
W – testis (male) – testosterone

B   slower, longer

C   X

What you need to remember

hormonal / endocrine, hormones, target, nervous, master

B11.2

A   glucose – the sugar used in respiration
glycogen – a storage carbohydrate found in the liver and muscles
insulin – a hormone that allows glucose to move from the blood into cells
pancreas – a gland that secretes insulin

B   Too much glucose in the blood. $\rightarrow$ The pancreas secretes insulin into the bloodstream. $\rightarrow$ Glucose moves from the blood into the cells. $\rightarrow$ Blood glucose levels decrease.

C   rare in children – type 2 diabetes
the most common form of diabetes – type 2 diabetes
the pancreas stops producing insulin – type 1 diabetes
body cells don't respond properly to insulin – type 2 diabetes
obesity is a risk factor – type 2 diabetes
becoming more common in the UK – type 2 diabetes

What you need to remember

pancreas, insulin, glycogen, 1, 2

B11.3

A a **X**

   b the blood glucose level of person **X** went up higher than that of person **Y** and it took more time to come back down to the starting level

B the blood glucose levels of a person with type 1 diabetes can be controlled using insulin and changes to their diet so it does not rise too high or too low; but they will always have the illness because the cells in their pancreas are damaged and this cannot be reversed

C **W** – Type 2

   X – Type 1, Type 2

   Y – n/a

   Z – Type 2

What you need to remember

insulin, carbohydrates, exercise, drugs

B11.4

A clockwise from top: fallopian tube, uterus, vagina, cervix, ovary

B testes – makes sperm

   scrotum – keeps the testes away from the body for maximum sperm production

   sperm duct – carries sperm to the penis

   penis – places sperm into the vagina

C **T, U**

D **W** – boys, girls

   X – girls

   Y – boys, girls

   Z – boys

What you need to remember

puberty, sexual, ovaries, ovulation, menstrual, follicle, progesterone, Testosterone, testes

B11.5

A contraceptive pill – **H**

   condoms – **B**

   vasectomy – **O**

   contraceptive implant – **H**

   diaphragm – **B**

B a false

   b true

   c true

   d true

C **Z**

What you need to remember

sperm, uterus, pill, sperm, Barrier, condoms, abstinence

B11 Practice questions

01.1 endocrine, glands, blood, effect [2]

01.2 oestrogen – main female reproductive hormone

   insulin – involved in the control of blood glucose levels

   testosterone – main male reproductive hormone

   FSH – causes eggs in the ovary to mature [2]

01.3 ovary [1]

02 during days 0-5 levels of all hormones are low and menstruation happens, [1] during which the unfertilised egg leaves the body along with the womb lining; [1] during days 0–12 FSH causes a new egg to mature in the ovary [1] and oestrogen levels climb, causing the thickness of the womb lining to increase in preparation to receive a fertilised egg; [1] at day 12 levels of LH are at their highest, causing an egg to be released from an ovary (ovulation); [1] between days 15–28 levels of oestrogen decrease whilst the thickness of the womb lining remains constant [1]

B12.1

A Genetic material is passed from parent to offspring. – asexual, sexual

   Involves two parents. – sexual

   The offspring are clones of the parent. – asexual

   The offspring are genetically different from each other. – sexual

   The offspring are formed by fertilisation. – sexual

   Requires sperm and egg cells in animals. – sexual

   Requires pollen and egg cells in flowering plants. – sexual

B a asexual

   b sexual

   c asexual

   d sexual

C **W**

What you need to remember

one, sex, identical, meiosis, sexual, variation

B12.2

A mitosis – cell division that produces identical cells

   meiosis – cell division that produces gametes

   gamete – a sex cell (sperm and egg in humans)

   fertilisation – the joining of a male and female sex cell

   gene – a section of DNA

B first row: **Y**

   second row: **X**

   third row: **Y, Y**

   fourth row: **Z, Z, Z, Z**

C skin cell 46

   sperm cell 23

   zygote 46

   egg cell 23

   ovary cell 46

What you need to remember

meiosis, two, divides, four, fertilisation, mitosis

B12.3

A DNA, chromosomes, genes

B gene **V**

   chromosome **U**

   cell **S**

   nucleus **T**

C **X**

D one from: to help cure genetic diseases either through medicines or by repairing the faulty genes, to help us understand human evolution and history

What you need to remember

polymer / molecule, double, chromosome, protein, genome

B12.4

A A section of DNA that codes for one protein. – gene

   Different forms of a gene. – allele

   An individual with two identical alleles for a characteristic. – homozygous

   An individual with different alleles for a characteristic. – heterozygous

   Made up of many amino acids joined together. – protein

   Describes the alleles that an individual has. – genotype

   Describes the physical appearance of an individual. – phenotype

B a heterozygous genotype – Hh

   a genotype for the phenotype curly hair – hh

   a homozygous dominant genotype – HH

What you need to remember

alleles, genotype, phenotype, same, heterozygous, dominant, recessive, two

B12.5

A a false

   b true

   c false

   d true

   e true

B male – XY

   female – XX

C people **6** and **7** both have free earlobes but they have a son (person **10**) who has attached earlobes; this means that they could both be carriers of the recessive allele and have passed on this allele to their son

What you need to remember

Punnett, phenotypes, ratios, 23, sex, X, males / men

B12.6

A polydactyly **V, 1**

   cystic fibrosis **U, 2**

   Huntington's disease **W, 1**

B **X, Y**

C lungs – reduction in oxygen reaching her bloodstream

   small intestine – difficulty digesting food

   fallopian tubes – fertility problems

What you need to remember

inherited, polydactyly, dominant, mucus, recessive, both

B12.7

A carried out between 10 and 12 weeks – chorionic villus sampling

carried out between 15 and 16 weeks – amniocentesis

needle inserted into the baby – n/a

needle inserted through the wall of the uterus – chorionic villus sampling, amniocentesis

cells taken from the placenta – chorionic villus sampling

cells taken from the amniotic fluid – amniocentesis

associated with a small risk of miscarriage – chorionic villus sampling, amniocentesis

B X, Y, V, Z, W

What you need to remember

fetuses, genes, villus, miscarriage, IVF, ethical

B12 Practice questions

01.1 sexual [1]

01.2 **A** – meiosis [1]

B – fertilisation [1]

01.3 zygote [1]

01.4 **X** – 46 [1]

Y – 23 [1]

Z – 46 [1]

02

Gametes	X	Y
X	**XX**	**XY**
X	XX	XY

[2]

the ratio of XX (female) to XY (male) is 1 : 1 **or** 50% probability of XX (female) and 50% XY (male) [1]

B13.1

A eye colour – genetics

height – a combination of both

accent – environment

pierced ears – environment

blood group – genetics

skin colour – a combination of both

B W, X, Z

C a no

b identical twins have the same genes; if type 1 diabetes was only due to genetics, if one twin had it then so would the other 100% of the time

What you need to remember

Variation, genes, environmental, both, twins, genetics, environment

B13.2

A U

B they will be able to see predators more quickly and escape before being eaten, they will be able to find more food

C mutation of a gene **X**

advantage to survival **W**

breed **Z**

pass on genes **Y**

What you need to remember

natural, billion, mutations, environmental, breed / reproduce, fertile, species

B13.3

A two from: large grains, many grains, short stalk (to prevent them being blown over by the wind), resistance to disease, resistance to insect attack

B select animals that have useful characteristics

C tomato plant – resistance to disease

dog – obedience

rose – brightly coloured flowers

pig – more muscle

D inbreeding, which causes little variation in the population, increasing the risk of certain diseases or inherited defects (e.g., breathing problems in pugs)

What you need to remember

animals, breed, resistance, gentle / obedient, flowers, variation

B13.4

A X

B make human proteins – bacteria, cows

more nutritional – crops

resistance to pests – crops

increase in yield – crops

C $\frac{58}{158} \times 100 = 36.7\%$

What you need to remember

engineering, gene, resistant, modified

B13.5

A N, P

B a T

b any inherited disorder (e.g., cystic fibrosis)

C W – R

X – B

Y – B

Z – R

What you need to remember

inherited, benefits, increase, risk, designer

B13 Practice questions

01.1 a GM crop has had its genetic material changed / has a gene from another organism [1]

01.2 100 – 62 – 4 = 34% [2]

01.3 bar drawn at 34% [1]

01.4 two from: possible effects of eating GM food on human health, genes from GM organisms may spread to wildlife, people might create 'designer' children, it is a new science and its long-term effects are unknown [2]

02.1 one from: temperature, volume of water given to plant, type of soil [1]

02.2 from 12.6 cm to 36.2 cm [1]

02.3 height – environmental [1]

the seedlings were all different heights; they have the same genes, so if it was genetic they would all be the same height [1]

colour of flower – genetic [1]

the seedlings all had the gene for white flowers [1]

B14.1

A a Charles Darwin

b X

B 2 – The flesh rots, leaving the skeleton.

4 – Over millions of years minerals replace the bone tissue.

1 – An animal dies and falls to the ground

3 – Layers of sediment build up over the skeleton.

C 1 000 000 years – 10^6 years

100 million years – 10^8 years

100 thousand years – 10^5 years

1 billion years – 10^9 years

What you need to remember

millions, rocks, decay, minerals, life, soft, geological

B14.2

A Y

B new disease – Australian Tasmanian devil dying from a form of communicable cancer

successful competition – rabbits in Australia breeding quickly

new predator – hedgehogs on North Uist eating seabird eggs

C a between the 17th and 20th centuries the number of extinctions in each century has increased, from 7 in the 17th century to 68 in the 20th century

b the human population has increased, so more natural habitat destroyed / more pollution

What you need to remember

fossils, Extinction, species, predators

B14.3

A circle – volcanic eruption, meteor hitting the Earth

B X

C a unexpected changes to fossils in Norway – decrease in temperature

huge crater in Chicxulub, Mexico – asteroid collision

layers of crater debris in rocks that are 65 million years old – asteroid collision fossil record shows tropical vegetation was replaced by woodland plants – decrease in temperature

lots of iridium under the crater in Mexico – asteroid collision

b at the moment there is more convincing evidence to support the asteroid collision than there is to support other theories

What you need to remember

volcanic, asteroids / meteors, mass, dinosaurs, evidence

B14.4

A antibiotics, less, cannot, mutations, survive, increases

B **S, T, U**

C a use antibacterial hand gel on way into hospital and on leaving

b wash hands well with antibacterial soap / gel in between examining patients; wear disposable clothing or clothing that is regularly sterilised

c only prescribe antibiotics for bacterial infections (not viral) when they are really needed; make sure the correct antibiotic is being used

d finish the whole course of antibiotics, even if they begin to feel better

What you need to remember

reproduce, antibiotics, MRSA, increases, doctors, expensive

B14.5

A **4** – species
1 – kingdom
3 – genus
2 – class

B **X, Y**

C species – *maritimus*
kingdom – animal
genus – *Ursus*

What you need to remember

Linnaeus, phylum, binomial, microscopes, classification

B14.6

A left column, top to bottom: domain, bacteria, eukaryota
right column, top to bottom: archaebacteria, plants, protista

B a eukaryota
b it contains a nucleus

C a false
b false
c true
d true
e false

What you need to remember

kingdom, bacteria, trees

B14 Practice questions

01.1 domains [1]
01.2 fungi [1]
01.3 **U, V** [2]
02.1 fossils [1]
02.2 **Z** [1]
02.3 the numbers are very big; [1] using standard form makes the large numbers easier to write and understand, minimising mistakes [1]
02.4 there are no fossils from this time [1] **plus** one reason why from: early organisms were soft-bodied so did not form fossils; fossils may have been destroyed by geological activity [1]

B15.1

A An ecosystem is made up of – organisms interacting with non-living elements of their environment.
A community is – populations of different species.
Interdependence is how – different organisms rely on each other for food, shelter, etc.
An abiotic factor is – a non-living factor.

B **Y**

C an example of how plants are dependent on animals – reproduction, source of food
an example of how animals are dependent on plants – source of food, source of materials for shelter

What you need to remember

ecosystem, food, seed, interdependence, stable

B15.2

A light intensity – abiotic
temperature – abiotic
a new pathogen – biotic
soil pH – abiotic
availability of food – biotic
competition between organisms – biotic

B a decrease, they will die of the disease
b increase, there are fewer ladybirds eating them
c decrease, there are fewer ladybirds for blue tits to eat so they will eat more caterpillars

What you need to remember

light, mineral, carbon dioxide, Biotic, food

B15.3

A quadrat

B **X, Y**

C $\frac{1}{0.25}$ = 4 quadrats in 1 square metre
$4 \times 9 = 36$ barnacles

What you need to remember

ecologists, biotic, population, distribution, Quadrats, transect

B15.4

A circle – a mate, food, territory

B they can eat more different types of food, so don't have to compete as much for food with other animals.

C brightly coloured tail feathers – attracting a mate
good eyesight – finding food
prickles – to avoid being eaten by predators
living in a pack – maintaining a territory

What you need to remember

mate, adapted, offspring, different

B15.5

A light – so they can photosynthesise and make food
space to grow – so their roots can take in enough water and minerals, and so their leaves can capture enough light
minerals from the soil – to make the chemicals they need for growth
water – so they can keep their tissues rigid

B dispersal, away from, reduces, light, space, increases

C The seeds that were spread out grew the most – **C**
Plant growth will be affected by how crowded they are – **H**
It is important to keep all other conditions the same – n/a
Plants that are close to each other have to compete more for resources – **E**

What you need to remember

compete, food / glucose, water, soil, adaptations

B15.6

A yeast (microscopic fungus) – oxygen, water, food
cactus (plant) – water, carbon dioxide, light
shark (animal) – oxygen, water, food

B high salt concentration – special cytoplasm in cells to stop water moving out by osmosis
high temperature – enzymes that are resistant to denaturation
low temperature – chemical in cells that acts like antifreeze

C a false
b true
c false
d false
e true

What you need to remember

adaptations, Extremophiles, temperature

B15.7

A migration to a warmer climate in the winter – behavioural

thick fur for insulation – structural

kidneys that produce very concentrated urine – functional

sleeping in cool burrows during the day – behavioural

camouflage – structural

B a circle – very little sweating; active only in the early morning and evening; large surface area to volume ratio; large, thin ears

b underline – small surface area to volume ratio; layer of blubber under the skin; thick fur coat; chemical that acts like antifreeze in cells

C a one from: large, thin ears; a large surface area to volume ratio

b thick fur coat

What you need to remember

structural, migration, functional

B15.8

A **X, Z**

B photosynthesis, leaves, carbon dioxide, stomata, evaporation, adaptations

C leaves are spines – reduces water loss

roots are spread over a wide area – increases uptake of water

stem stores water – so water is available at all times

What you need to remember

decrease, spines, root, water

B15 Practice questions

01.1 15×7 [1] = 105 (m²) [1]

01.2 **T, V** [2]

01.3 1 [1]

01.4 $0 + 1 + 3 + 0 + 2 + 1 + 3 + 1 + 1 + 2 = 14$ [1]

$\dfrac{14}{10} = 1.4$ [1]

01.5 **X** [1]

B16.1

A a box – birch tree, rose bush

b underline – Zara (human), butterfly, Milo (cat)

c star – butterfly

d C – Milo (cat)

e circle – Zara (human), Milo (cat)

B tomato plant → aphid → ladybird → blue tit → hawk

C a solid line – rabbits; dashed line – foxes

b **Y, Z**

What you need to remember

algae, producer, consumers, tertiary, predators

B16.2

A 2 – The animal dies.

1 – Plant material is eaten by an animal.

5 – Plants take up mineral ions through their roots.

4 – Mineral ions are released into the soil.

3 – Decomposers break down the dead body.

B evaporation – water changes from a liquid into vapour

transpiration – loss of water from plant leaves

condensation – water changes from vapour into a liquid

precipitation – falling of liquid water to the surface of the Earth

C from top to bottom: precipitation, condensation, transpiration, evaporation

What you need to remember

decomposition / decay, soil, cycle, precipitated

B16.3

A a respiration

b feeding

c photosynthesis

d combustion

B from top to bottom: photosynthesis, combustion, respiration, feeding

C the amount of carbon dioxide removed from the atmosphere by photosynthesis and the amount entering the atmosphere by respiration was the same

What you need to remember

cycle, fuels, decay / decomposition, carbon dioxide, photosynthesis, eat

B16 Practice questions

01.1 **T** [1]

01.2 **A** – feeding / eating [1]

B – photosynthesis [1]

C – combustion / burning [1]

01.3 **Y** [1]

01.4 decay /decomposition of dead organisms and waste [1] releases carbon dioxide into the atmosphere through respiration [1]

01.5 it is colder / temperature is lower in the Arctic; [1] rate of photosynthesis is lower [1]

01.6 470 billion tonnes of carbon dioxide is removed from the atmosphere (by photosynthesis); [1] 460 + 50 = 510 billion tonnes is released into the atmosphere (by respiration and combustion); [1] so there is an overall increase in the amount of carbon dioxide in the atmosphere [1] of 40 billion tonnes [1]

B17.1

A **Z**

B a decrease in biodiversity; there is now only one species of tree, which also limits the number of different animal species that can live in the forest, as not

all will be able to survive with just the oil palms as a source of food/shelter

b decrease in biodiversity; insect species will be killed, which will also cause a decrease in the populations of animals that eat the insects as they will have no food

C a 3 billion

b it will continue to increase

c we don't know what will happen in the future; the population is currently increasing but this increase may not continue at the same rate due to events that we can't predict

What you need to remember

Biodiversity, waste, high, reducing / decreasing, increasing, resources

B17.2

A nuclear weapon testing – radioactive waste

farming – pesticides in waterways

household waste – toxic chemicals spreading from landfill sites

human bodily waste – sewage

B 2 – Algae and water plants in the pond grow rapidly.

5 – The pond contains no life - it is 'dead'.

3 – Plants and algae die and are decayed by microorganisms that use oxygen from the water.

4 – Oxygen levels in the water fall rapidly – animals in the pond cannot survive.

1 – Fertilisers are washed from the soil and enter the pond.

C a **Y**

b **Z**

c **X**

d **Z**

What you need to remember

chemicals, water, fertilisers, reduce / decrease

B17.3

A a convertors

b less

c dimming

B a smog

b carbon dioxide

c particulates

d lungs

e sulfur dioxide

f fossil

What you need to remember

air / atmosphere, fuels, rain, dimming

B17.4

A a one from: trees are cut down and not replaced; animal species lose shelter and food source

b fewer trees to remove carbon dioxide from the atmosphere; trees are burnt, which releases carbon dioxide c to increase the amount of land for farming; to build new roads / homes; to supply wood for building

B a 4 100 000 − 3 331 065 = 768 935 (km²)

b $\frac{768\,935}{4\,100\,000} \times 100 = 18.75\%$

C a false

b true

c false

d true

e true

What you need to remember

trees, decayed, reduces / decreases, carbon dioxide

B17.5

A a the amount of carbon dioxide in the atmosphere increased between 1950 and 2010

b one from: the human population has increased, so more fossil fuels are being burnt in vehicles / power stations and carbon dioxide is released; trees are being cut down (deforestation) to provide land for farming and homes, so less carbon dioxide is being removed from the atmosphere

B Y – energy transferred from the Sun

W – energy absorbed by greenhouse gases in the atmosphere

Z – energy reflected and transferred into space

X – energy reradiated back to Earth

C rising sea levels – loss of biodiversity in low-lying areas

change in seasons – animals migrate at different times of the year

less rain in some areas – the distribution of plants will change

increase in Arctic temperatures – populations of animals adapted to cold climates will reduce

What you need to remember

methane, warming, sea, migration

B17.6

A W – ✗

X – ✓

Y – ✓

Z – ✗

B a underline – To build landfill sites large areas of land have to be cleared. This could be waste ground or it could be land that is habitat to many plants and animals.

b circle – When the rubbish is in the ground some chemicals can leak out of the rubbish and enter the land or waterways.

c one from: recycle more, reuse items (e.g., plastic bags), buy items that have less packaging, put organic waste into a compost bin

C between 2004 and 2010, the landfill tax rose from around £18/tonne to £50/tonne; in the same period, the amount of rubbish going to landfill decreased from around 8 million tonnes to 5 million tonnes

What you need to remember

breeding, hedgerows, resources

B17 Practice questions

01 carbon dioxide – global warming [1]
sulfur dioxide – acid rain [1]

02.1 as the global average surface temperature rises, so does the global average sea level [1]

02.2 the rise in temperatures causes the polar ice caps to melt, [1] so there is more water in the oceans [1]

02.3 low-lying areas are at risk of flooding, [1] reducing biodiversity, [1] because fewer organisms can live in this changed habitat [1]

03.1 four from: place each dish in an area with the same light intensity, place each dish in an area with the same temperature, give each dish the same volume of water / acid, use more than three seeds in each dish, make sure the seeds are spread out [4]

03.2 points plotted correctly; [2] line of best fit drawn [1]

03.3 yes, [1] because as the concentration of acid increased, the percentage of seeds that had germinated decreased [1]